The First Explorers of the Oceans

Unit 1

I. Pre-reading

1. Look at the world map below and locate the Atlantic, the Indian, and the Pacific Oceans.
2. Describe the voyage of Christopher Columbus from Spain to the West Indies.
3. Can you name anyone in the history of exploration who discovered or reached some place "first"?

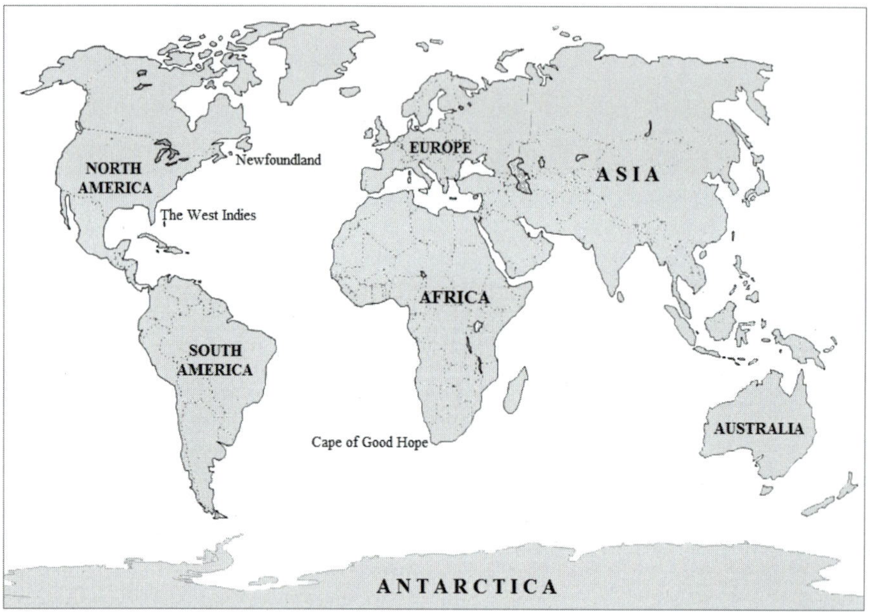

II. Vocabulary Preview

The following words appear in **bold** in the reading. Match each with its correct definition.

1. exploit	a. to go around something; encircle
2. hemisphere	b. a heroic or notable act
3. round	c. to discover or dig up something in the ground
4. settlement	d. a place where people come to live
5. steer	e. to direct the course of a ship or automobile
6. unearth	f. a half of a spherical body; a half of the earth divided by the equator

READINGS in OCEAN TOPICS

Hong Ok-Sook · Jhang Se-Eun
Lee Gunsoo · Noh Jongjin
Kevin Parent · Ryoo Mi-Lim

KYUNG MOON SA

READINGS in **OCEAN TOPICS**

ISBN 979-11-6073-396-9

KM KYUNG MOON SA
174, Wausan-ro Mapo-gu Seoul, Korea
Tel: (82) 2 332 2004
Fax: (82) 2 336 5193

Printed in Korea

Price ₩ 14,000

Contents

Unit 1 The First Explorers of the Oceans · 5

Unit 2 How Does a Ship Know Where It Is? · 15

Unit 3 Beautiful Ports of the World · 25

Unit 4 Whales around the Seas of Korea · 35

Unit 5 Ocean Life · 47

Unit 6 Aquaculture as an Alternative Way of Our Well-being · 57

Unit 7 The Dark Side of Technology · 69

Unit 8 How to Fly Underwater · 79

Unit 9 Coral Reefs, Lifeblood of Marine Life · 89

Unit 10 Marine Pollution: Oil Spill Incidents · 99

Unit 11 Island Tourism and Its Problems · 111

Unit 12 The Fourth Industrial Revolution and Autonomous Ships · 121

Answers · 133

Readings in Ocean Topics

III. Reading

The First Explorers of the Oceans

We usually think the great oceans of the world were explored by Europeans during **the Age of Exploration**[1] when adventurous seafarers risked their lives in search of **terra incognita**.[2] A deeper examination of their adventures, however, reveals economic motifs behind the **expeditions**. At first, the Portuguese and Spanish attempted to find a new maritime route to India and **the Spice Islands**[3] in order to obtain **spices**, which were highly desired but expensive and difficult to acquire. Because land routes to India were often dangerous or closed due to wars, traders faced adversities. Therefore, finding an alternative trade route was especially important for maritime countries such as Portugal and Spain because of the potential for enormous profit and wealth. Thus we know about the adventures of Europeans which eventually led to geographical discoveries which changed world history forever. However, it can be argued that they were not the first to perform the **exploits** of ocean crossing.

Most people could answer the question, "Who discovered the Americas?" It was Christopher Columbus who supposedly discovered the Americas. When he set out on his westward voyage under the sponsorship of the Spanish crown, he discovered the West Indies in 1492. The idea that he had set foot on a huge continent facing the Atlantic Ocean between Europe and India did not occur to him. Even after he visited the West Indies several times, he still firmly believed he had reached India.

There may have been several expeditions to the Americas prior to Columbus. Native Americans migrated from Asia in the prehistoric age when they unintentionally crossed the Bering Strait and reached North America in search of food. Their migration, however, cannot be considered an expedition. On the

1) **The Age of Exploration or Discovery:** The era between the early 15th century and the 17th century in which Europeans began exploring the world by sea in search of new trading routes.

2) **Terra incognita:** "unknown land" in Latin, a term used in cartography for regions that have not been mapped or documented.

3) **The Spice Islands:** The Indonesian archipelago of the Moluccas (or Maluku Islands) introduced to Europeans as the Spice Islands by Arab merchants, because spices like the nutmeg, mace, and cloves were exclusively found there.

other hand, some medieval Nordic **sagas** speak of Vikings led by Leif Erickson (c.970-1020) who sailed to "Vinland" across the ocean. Based on these legends, archeologists including Helge and Anne Stine Ingstad discovered ruined **settlements** on the coast of Newfoundland, Canada in the 1960s.

Although the Nordic settlement **unearthed** in Newfoundland did not bear physical resemblance to "Vinland" — "wine land" in Old Nordic language as described in the sagas, there is no doubt that the Vikings did indeed reach North America across the North Atlantic around 1000 A.D. almost five centuries prior to Columbus. The Viking expedition to "Vinland" seems to have been motivated by an attempt to find a new trade network.

The desire to pioneer a direct trade route to India by sea also **steered** Portuguese explorer Vasco da Gama (c.1460-1524) into voyage. Unlike Columbus who voyaged westward, he chose to follow the route taken by Bartolomeu Dias (c.1451-1500). Dias sailed down the west coast of Africa to the Cape of Good Hope, the southern tip of Africa, thus becoming the first European to thereby prove the Atlantic and Indian Oceans were connected. After sailing around the Cape of Good Hope, da Gama, on his voyage, continued further into the Indian Ocean, arriving at the city of Calicut, India in 1498, four months after his departure.

Arguably, however, the Portuguese explorer may not have been the first to **round** Africa. Herodotus, an ancient Greek historian, records the **circumnavigation** of Africa by the fleet of Necho II of Egypt. Aided by Phoenicians, who were known to be excellent seafarers, the Egyptian fleet started out from the Red Sea, following south along the east coast of Africa in 600 B.C. After rounding the Cape, they headed north to eventually enter the Mediterranean before reaching home. It took two years for the fleet to arrive at the Pillars of Hercules (the Straits of Gibraltar) and another year, to return home, for the sailors had to support themselves. They stopped each autumn at suitable places to sow wheat and wait for the next harvest. There are people who doubt this voyage really took place because there are no reliable records or proof from Egyptians besides the description from Herodotus. He wrote in a questioning manner, "As they sailed on a westerly course the southern end of **Libya**[4], they had the sun on their right—to northward of them." This record indicates that the sailors would have been in the southern **hemisphere**. The ancient people including Herodotus would not have understood this story because they believed the southern part of Africa was connected to Asia, and moreover, the idea of the southern

---

4) **Libya:** a republic in North Africa between Tunisia and Egypt; however in ancient Greek use, sometimes meaning all of Africa

hemisphere was entirely unheard of.

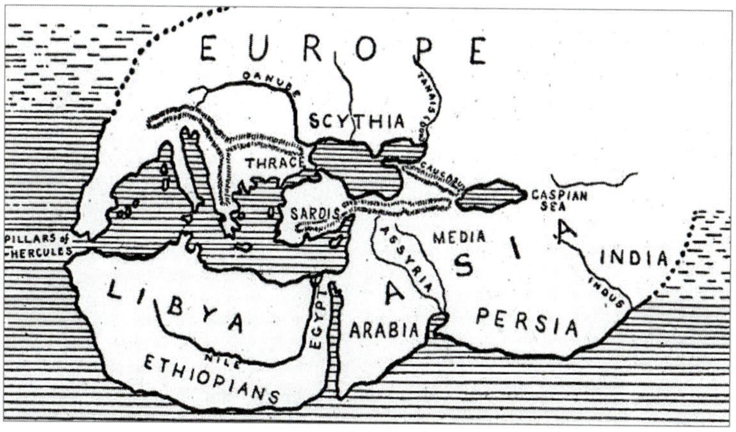

The world according to Herodotus

In Asia, the great voyage of the Chinese naval explorer Zheng He (1371-1433) preceded that of Columbus as well as Vasco da Gama. In 1405, his fleet of more than 27,000 men and more than 250 vessels (the largest ones having nine masts and measuring more than 120 meters long and 51 meters wide) sailed via the South China Sea, Champa (Vietnam), Java, Malacca, and Ceylon to Calicut, India. His seven expeditions which lasted until 1433 covered the entire Indian Ocean, reaching as far as the east coast of Africa. The purpose of the voyages was to display Ming China's glory and power and collect **tributes**.

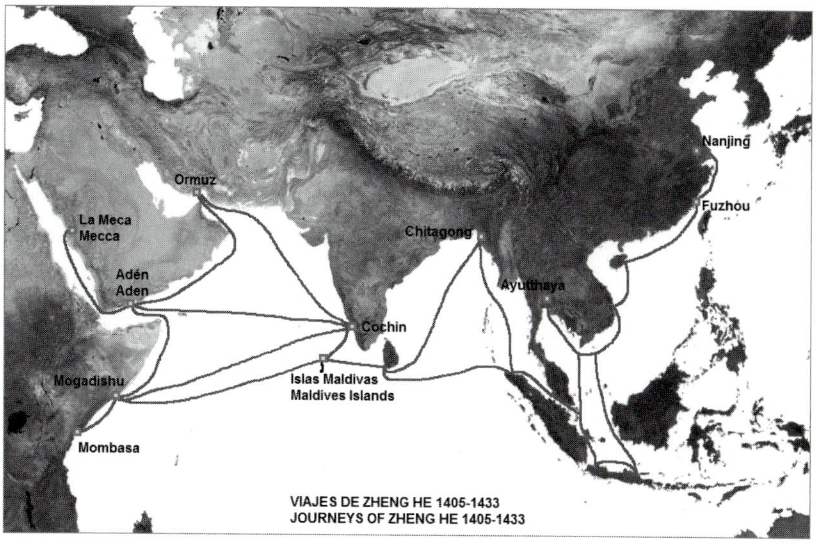

IV. Fact Check

Read the passage again and then read the following statements. Write a T if the statement is true and an F if false. If false, rewrite it to make it true.

1. _____ The Spaniards succeeded in trading with the Indian people through the maritime route.

2. _____ Land routes to India existed before the sea route to India was discovered.

3. _____ Erickson's expedition was recorded in the Nordic sagas.

4. _____ Vasco da Gama was the first European to reach the Cape of Good Hope.

5. _____ Herodotus is the first Greek that rounded Africa.

V. Reading Comprehension

Choose the best answer for each question.

1. What is the main idea of the text?
   a. Europeans played an important role in shaping the world history.
   b. Asians and Africans were the first explorers of the oceans.
   c. The 'first' voyages actually happened much earlier than we know.
   d. India was the destination of many Europeans' voyages.

2. Which of the following is TRUE about the route to India?

a. Europeans were looking for an alternative route to India.

b. The land route to India was closed due to no demand for spices.

c. Erickson also attempted to find a sea route in order to trade with India.

d. Columbus was the only one to have attempted the maritime route to India.

3. What is the significance of the voyage of Bartolomeu Dias?

a. Dias succeeded in arriving in India by land.

b. Dias was the first European to set out westward to reach India.

c. Dias was the first European to circumnavigate Africa.

d. Dias proved the Atlantic was connected to the Indian.

4. What can be inferred from the record of Herodotus?

a. Herodotus believed in the idea that the Earth is round.

b. Herodotus copied the event of the voyage from an Egyptian source.

c. Herodotus thought Africa was connected to India.

d. Herodotus somehow doubted the story he recorded.

5. Choose the statement which is NOT correct about Zheng He's expedition.

a. He arrived at Calicut earlier than Vasco da Gama.

b. His fleet sailed westward as far as the Pillars of Hercules.

c. The expedition was intended to boast political power of China.

d. His first expedition covered mostly up to the eastern half of the Indian.

VI. Developing Reading Skills

Finding the Main Idea of a Paragraph

An important skill for reading is finding the main idea. The main idea of a paragraph is the author's message about the topic and is often presented in partial form near the beginning, expanded upon in the middle, and stated more directly at the end of the writing. The sentence that states the main idea is called a topic sentence. The topic sentence, if not always, tends to be the first sentence in a paragraph. Keep in mind that the main idea is sometimes not clearly stated but implied.

VII. Vocabulary in Context

1. Fill in the blank with the **boldfaced** word or phrase from the reading that best completes each sentence. Change the form of the word if necessary.

(1) Chile and Australia are located on the southern ____________ of the Earth.

(2) The conquered countries had to pay __________ to their conqueror as a token of submission.

(3) Tolkien's *Lord of the Rings* trilogy owes a lot to the Nordic _________.

2. Choose a word or phrase that best completes each sentence.

(1) _______ built by the prehistoric people was discovered by archeologists.

a. settle　b. settling　c. settlement　d. settlements

(2) The _______ of Roald Amundsen was that he first reached the South Pole in 1911.

a. execution　b. experiment　c. exploitation　d. exploit

(3) We chose the route to ________ the island.

a. circumstance　b. circumnavigate

c. circumscribe　d. circumspect

VIII. Grammar Point

Spanish or Spaniard?

Spanish refers to both a language as a noun and people as an adjective. A Spaniard is a person who is from Spain or speaks Spanish. You can say "a Spanish person" or you could just say "a Spaniard."

English or British? The United Kingdom (UK) consists of England, Scotland, Wales and Northern Ireland, while (Great) Britain refers to the territory of England, Scotland, and Wales. Scottish or Welsh or Northern Irish people would not like to be called English due to the complicated historical conflicts among England and their country. Although English is limited to the people living in England, British may mean the people living in the UK. English, however, also means the language spoken by all of these people.

IX. Writing a Summary

A summary is a short paragraph that provides the most important information from a reading. It usually includes the main ideas, not details. When you write a summary, don't copy from the reading. Use your own words.

Write a summary of the passage. It should not be more than five sentences. The first sentences of the summary are given below. Write two or three more sentences to complete the summary.

We usually think the first explorers of the world oceans were Europeans during the Age of Exploration. However, there have been explorers before those who were known to be the first explorers.

____

____

____

____

X. Topics for Discussion and Writing

Look at the map and describe the routes of following voyages to your partner. Then write them down.

1. Ancient Egyptians' circumnavigation route of Africa
2. Vasco da Gama's voyage to India
3. Zheng He's route on his first voyage

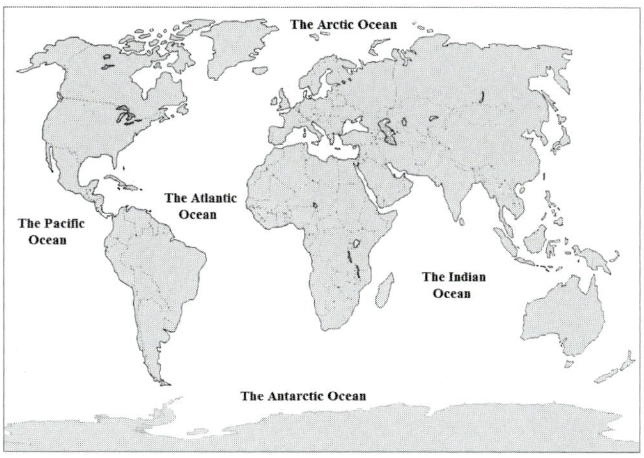

Did You Know?

Who was the first European to discover the Pacific Ocean? Ferdinand Magellan (c. 1480 – 1521), a Portuguese explorer, wanted to find the western sea route to India and the Spice Islands. He set out from Spain with a fleet of five ships in 1519. He went down the Atlantic and navigated through the sea route which is known as the Strait of Magellan at the southern tip of South America. He became the first European to find and cross the Pacific Ocean, which he named. He died on the voyage and only 18 out of the original 270 crew members could return home in 1522.

How Does a Ship Know Where It Is?

Unit 2

I. Pre-reading

1. When was the last time you used GPS?
2. Have you ever had an experience where the GPS did not give you good directions?
3. If you woke up alone in a small boat, how could you tell which direction you were facing?
4. Have you ever been lost? What happened and how did it feel?

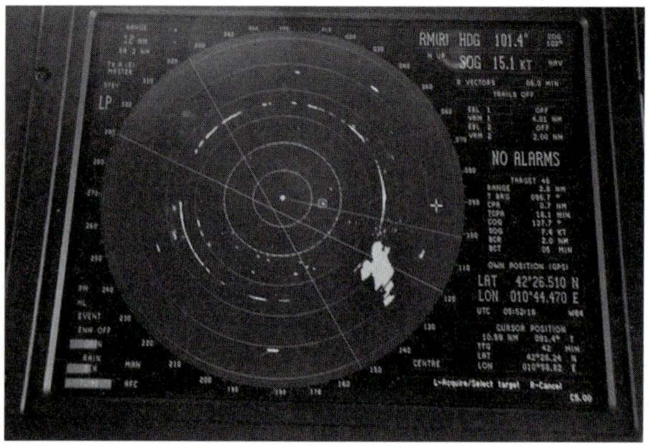

Block II/IIA/IIR/IIR-M satellite (Source: USAF)

II. Vocabulary Preview

The following words appear in **bold** in the reading. Match each with its correct definition.

1. celestial body	a. occurring with a regular degree of frequency
2. buffet	b. to hit or push repeatedly
3. predecessor	c. a natural object located outside the Earth's atmosphere
4. orient	d. that which comes before
5. routinely	e. to determine one's position or direction when this is previously unknown
6. constellation	f. a group of stars that appears to form a pattern or picture like Orion the Great Hunter

III. Reading

How Does a Ship Know Where It Is?

Driving to a new location without using GPS has become almost unthinkable, but so long as we know which streets to take and which corners to turn at, we will reach our destination. The ocean, however, doesn't have roads or corners; it is one great expanse of never-ending blue. How could the ancient mariners successfully navigate their journey from one continent to another? Once you travel far enough and can no longer see land, simply pointing your ship in a certain direction was insufficient. Waves, winds and storms would blow you off-course every day of a journey that might take two months to complete. How could they complete their journeys?

Often they did not. Ships were **routinely** lost at sea, and the ocean floor is peppered with their sunken remains. Even those who successfully reached their destinations were constantly battling the elements and realigning their ship with the stars.

Navigation by the stars was no easy task. Directions could be ascertained from the **constellations**, but some constellations (for example, the twelve zodiac constellations) can only be seen in the northern hemisphere, and others only in the south. Further, some constellations are seasonal and therefore only visible at certain times of the year. And stars are usually not visible in a storm, and as a ship is being blown off-course, the crew may not know which way they are facing until after the storm has passed. In addition to the knowledge required to use the stars in this manner, knowing which way is north and which way is west may get you from Europe to North America, but it's still a challenge to get from Southampton in the UK to Port Newark, USA using the stars alone.

The first compasses were invented in China around 2000 years ago, centuries after humans began traversing the oceans of the Earth. Originally, these were used for fortune-telling, and it was only later that seafaring people began to recognise their value to navigation. It wasn't until the thirteenth century that they became standard equipment on ships.

The introduction of the compass solved some of the problems. It required less knowledge of the world's skies (though this was still necessary for successful navigation) and could be used during daylight, but it still only told you which direction you were facing. If you were traveling to Asia or Africa, you could be sure you were heading in the right direction, but you probably wouldn't know where you were in relation to the port you intended to visit.

In the tenth century, the Arab world introduced two tools that became very important to navigators: the quadrant and the astrolabe. The quadrant was so-named because it was one-fourth of a circle. Users would hold it, aligning it to both the sun (or another **celestial body**) and the horizon to measure the altitude of the sun. An astrolabe could be used to identify stars and the local latitude. Together, ship's navigators could determine their position according to the latitudinal and longitudinal standards. Therefore, by knowing the coordinates of their destination, they could determine, with some mathematical calculation, how to steer towards their intended destination.

Over time, the quadrant was refined and replaced with the octant (one-eighth of a circle) and finally the sextant (one-sixth of a circle). The sextant can measure up to 120°, as opposed to the 90° provided by the octant. As such, the sextant not only provides more information to the navigator but is a smaller instrument, an important improvement when ocean winds are **buffeting** the ship. Together with the ship's chronometer and an **almanac**, navigators could pinpoint their locations.

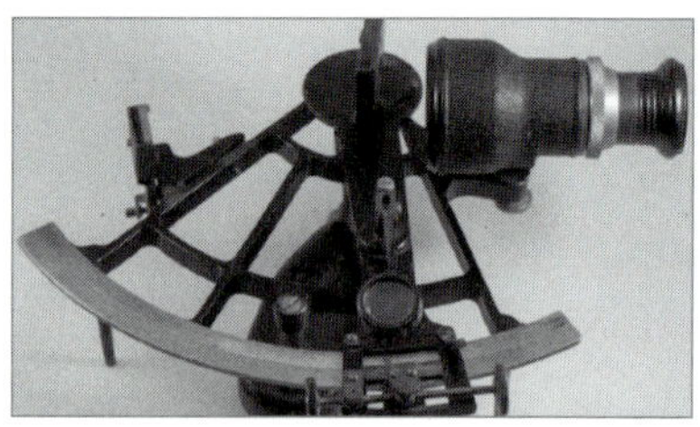

Scientific advances in the late 1800s allowed communication between ships and stations. This had previously only been via signals such as semaphore (a system of signalling involving a person holding a flag in each hand). The twentieth century saw many more navigational innovations, including the radio beacon. These structures transmit electronic signals on specified frequencies, allowing ships to use radio-direction tools to determine the distance and **orientation** to the beacon.

The development of the Global Positioning System occurred some 40 years ago. The principle is not significantly different from its **predecessors**. Instead of having to view a celestial body such as the sun or a stationary structure like a beacon, satellites orbiting the Earth transmit their coordinates, allowing on-board computers to calculate their own position on the planet. The reason we now have this technology in our pockets is related to the tragic loss of Korean Air flight 007. That airplane flew off-course in 1983 because of a navigational error and wandered into prohibited Soviet airspace where it was shot down. Although GPS had been in use since 1978, it was not available to Korean Air nor to anyone outside the US military; however, following the shooting down of the Korean passenger plane, then-US president Ronald Reagan declared that the Global Positioning System would be made available without charge to civilians. Now, not only will all ships and airplanes know exactly where they are, but GPS is readily available to anybody with a phone.

IV. Fact Check

Read the passage again and then read the following statements. Write a T if the statement is true and an F if false. If false, rewrite it to make it true.

1. _____ GPS became available to civilians because of the shot down of Korean Air airplane.

2. _____ An octant is twice the size of a quadrant.

3. _____ In pre-computer days, a ship's navigator needed to be good at mathematics.

4. _____ The astrolabe was developed in China.

5. _____ Using two flags to communicate from one ship to another is called semaphore.

V. Reading Comprehension

Choose the best answer for each question.

1. A nautical structure that may use radio waves is ______________.
   a. satellite
   b. beacon
   c. semaphore
   d. sextant

2. One problem with using stars to navigate is ______________.
   a. stars are not always visible
   b. stars are not always in the same position
   c. stars seldom leave Hollywood
   d. none of the above

3. The sextant ______________.
   a. was developed in China
   b. is not as good as an octant
   c. can measure right angles only
   d. none of the above

4. Korean Air flight 007 ______________.
   a. helped the development of the sextant
   b. transported Ronald Reagan to the US
   c. contributed to the reason GPS is available on our cell phones
   d. was scheduled to fly to the Soviet Union

5. Radio beacons ______________.
   a. are a two-way communication
   b. are held by the ship's navigator
   c. transmit frequencies which ships can use
   d. provide soothing music in the rough ocean.

VI. Vocabulary in Context

1. Fill in the blank with the **boldfaced** word or phrase from the reading that best completes each sentence. Change the form of the word if necessary.

(1) Flowers usually ______________ themselves towards the sun.

(2) The small port city had been constantly ______________ by winds and waves.

(3) He ______________ left the house at 7:17am.

2. Choose a word or phrase that best completes each sentence.

(1) The sun and moon are the two most important ______________ that influence human life.

a. celestial bodies

b. buffets

c. predecessors

d. almanac

(2) The navigator consulted the ____________ to determine the time when the moon would be directly overhead.

a. almanac

b. radio beacon

c. hemisphere

d. internet

(3) The recent typhoon ____________ Busan for several days.

a. navigated

b. buffeted

c. oriented

d. signalled

VIII. Grammar Point

Some words have different meanings. In some cases, the relationship between the meanings, or senses, is obvious. For example, when we use black pepper on our food, we can say we have peppered our food, and similarly, we can say the ocean floor is peppered with wrecked ships. It doesn't mean it is completely covered with ruins, but there are many of them. Some words, however, are completely unrelated, such as *school*, which, in addition to the meaning you already know, can also refer to a group (or shoal) of fish.

But sometimes the meanings are related, but the relationship is not obvious.

The word *course* refers to both the route taken by a ship and a class you take in university. This is not a coincidence as the meanings are related, though the relationship may not be immediately obvious. Do you see any connection between the two meanings?

What is the commonality between a ship orienting itself to a star and a freshman orientation session at a university?

IX. Writing a Summary

A summary is a short paragraph that provides the most important information from a reading. It usually includes the main ideas, not details. When you write a summary, don't copy from the reading. Use your own words.

Write a summary of the passage. It should not be more than five sentences. The first two sentences of the summary are below. Write two or three more sentences to complete the summary.

Ships traversing the oceans did not always rely on GPS to know where they were. Several inventions were developed to assist navigators in arriving at their intended destination.

X. Topics for Discussion and Writing

1. How has a recent invention changed your life, or the lives of others?

2. How different would the world be today if GPS was still only used by the military and ambulance drivers?

Did You Know?

When you don't know a word, you may find doing a google image search more helpful than a dictionary. This is especially true with concrete nouns like *sextant*, *astrolabe*, etc.

Readings in Ocean Topics

Beautiful Ports of the World

Unit 3

I. Pre-reading

1. What do you think these cities have in common?
2. What do you usually look for when you visit a city?
3. What do you think are the important things a port city must have to be considered beautiful?

II. Vocabulary Preview

The following words appear in **bold** in the reading. Match each with its correct definition.

1. liberal	a. to cross a body of water on or as in a canoe
2. ethnic	b. sound of rapid vibration
3. flock	c. to gather together or go in large numbers
4. buzz	d. to control, govern, or rule by superior authority
5. dominate	e. showing or characterized by broad-mindedness
6. ferry	f. belonging to a national group by heritage or culture
7. vibrant	g. vigorous, lively with energy or activity

III. Reading

Beautiful Ports of the World

There are many beautiful ports worldwide. Not only do they function as ports where diverse types of vessels dock, load and unload cargo, but they also draw millions of tourists because of their beauty. Tourists may argue over which port provides the most beautiful view or offers the best convenience for visitors, and the debate could be lengthy. Discovering some of the world's most beautiful ports, as described below, may narrow that debate. They all have their unique characteristics, as well as diverse merits, to be considered the most beautiful ports.

Firstly, New York, also known as the Big Apple: It may not be considered by many as one of the most beautiful port cities. However, it attracts innumerable tourists all year round. It is a **liberal** and multicultural city with people from all over the world. Its diverse **ethnic** groups and people of different cultures make the city one of the most desirable destinations for a visit. Millions upon millions of visitors **flock** to this city every year as there are numerous tourist attractions and sites. New York city, home to more than eight million people, offers unforgettable experiences at every step of its various districts, including impressive skyscrapers and famous corporate buildings, as well as a number of famous museums and galleries throughout the city, such as the Museum of Modern Art, the Guggenheim Museum and the Metropolitan Museum of Art. It is, without a doubt, a renowned cultural hub.
Manhattan is the heart and soul of the city and within its neighborhoods there is a distinct style and pace. Lower Manhattan, the city's financial district, is a **buzz** from Monday to Friday. The neon lights of Times Square and Broadway burn brightly in Midtown, while **dominating** the Upper East and West sides are Central Park, high-end boutiques and those famous brownstone homes. If you make your way down to New York harbor and jump on a **ferry** to Liberty Island, you will encounter the world famous Statue of Liberty, or Lady Liberty as she is often called.

On the other side of the world, Sydney is famous for having one of the world's most famous and beautiful harbors. As a gate-way to the Pacific Ocean, Sydney is also a **vibrant**, cosmopolitan city with a diverse population and a rich history. It is a magnificent place to visit, especially if you arrive at the city-center by cruise ship. Sydney attracts a tremendous number of visitors into the heart of the city with its **exhilarating** scene of the spectacular Sydney Opera House and impressive Harbour Bridge. The city

also has an array of beautiful beaches and national parks that offer a taste of Sydney's enviable outdoors scenery and lifestyle.

The uniqueness of Venice has been **enchanting** people for centuries, with its **shimmering** canals dotted with **gondolas**[1)] and bridges that meander through the city instead of roadways. It is famous for its sheer loveliness, as an **exquisite** city that seems to be miraculously built on water. As one of the most popular Mediterranean major shipping ports in maritime history, it is a city of gothic-style architecture with Byzantine and Arab influences. The cityscape, artistic cultural heritage, and luxurious establishments furnish it as one of the world's most popular tourist destinations.

Istanbul, Turkey, is the city where East meets West. Historically known firstly as Byzantium and then as Constantinople until early in the 20th century, Istanbul is the largest city and the cultural, economic, and financial center of Turkey. As one of the oldest ports in maritime history, and geographically considered as one of the major shipping ports; the Sea of Marmara, the Golden Horn, the Black Sea and the Bosphorus surround the city from all sides, Istanbul is full of majestic places to explore. The city **spellbinds** visitors with famous landmarks as it hosts a unique cultural and architectural heritage illustrated by the 6th-century Hagia Sophia and the 17th-century Blue Mosque. A short trip from the port to the old city allows tourists the opportunity to visit to opulent museums, palaces, churches, mosques, as well as bazaars where high quality carpets, leather goods, jewelry, and antique reproductions are readily available at reasonable prices.

Moving on to the Greek island of Santorini, we discover a place praised more for its breathtaking natural beauty than for its beaches. Although Santorini is a barren volcanic island, it is a stunning picture of whitewashed houses,

---

1) **Gondola:** A long, narrow, flat-bottomed boat having a tall, ornamental stem and stern and sometimes a small cabin for passenger, rowed by a single person who stands at the stern, facing forward.

multi-hued cliffs and charming bougainvillea-lined streets that also happens to have some of the best views of the Mediterranean Sea. Santorini is an incredibly popular port for Mediterranean cruises, offering memorable experiences for tourists to reach Fira, the main town, by cable car, mule ride or on foot.

Lastly, we determine that Rio de Janeiro, the largest coastal city in Brazil, deserves its position as one of the world's most beautiful port cities. Made famous by Christ the Redeemer, the massive statue of Jesus Christ that overlooks the city, the city's mountainous surroundings and shoreline can be enjoyed from below, at the base of the statue itself, or above from a cable car. A considerable number of geographical features can be found throughout the coastal areas of Rio, such as picturesque islands, reefs, bays and beaches. Cruise ships sail into Guanabara Bay past the city's famous beaches, before **skirting** the dramatic outcrop of Sugarloaf Mountain and docking just beyond the city center, where the beautiful **marinas**[2)] and mountains meet.

Clearly the port cities illustrated here all possess grandeur and charm, each unique to themselves. We do, however, find culture, history, diversity and natural beauty in all of them. Which one do you prefer?

IV. Fact Check

Read the passage again and then read the following statements. Write a T if the statement is true and an F if false. If false, rewrite it to make it true.

1. _____ New York is the port that attracts the most Asians.

2. _____ Venice is famous for its canals and bridges.

3. _____ Each of the world's famous ports has an iconic building.

4. _____ Santorini has many whitewashed buildings and charming bougainvillealined streets.

2) **Marina:** A boat basin offering dockage and other service for small craft.

5. _____ Istanbul as one of the major shipping ports hosts a unique cultural and architectural heritage.

V. Reading Comprehension

Choose the best answer for each question.

1. Which of the following is NOT a correct statement about the ports described?
   a. New York is also called the Big Apple.
   b. Venice was a very popular port because of its location.
   c. Istanbul used to be known as Byzantium and Constantinople.
   d. Rio de Janeiro is famous for its steep seafront cliffs.

2. What is NOT true about Manhattan of New York city?
   a. It is the heart and soul of the city.
   b. It has a distinct style and pace of life within its neighborhoods.
   c. Midtown is famous for Central Park.
   d. It is the city's financial district where a lot of corporate buildings are located.

3. What is the main purpose of this reading?
   a. To introduce some of the most beautiful and important ports of the world
   b. To compare the function of the most beautiful ports of the world
   c. To rank and compare the sizes of the most beautiful ports of the world
   d. To plan a visit to the most exciting ports of the world

4. Which continent is NOT mentioned in the reading?
   a. Europe b. Oceania c. America d. Africa

5. Which popular tourist activity is NOT mentioned in the reading?
   a. Viewing a statue
   b. Visiting museums and palaces
   c. Spending time at a beach
   d. Watching a volcanic eruption

VI. Developing Reading Skills

Identifying sequential words or phrases

Writers usually include some sequential words or phrases so that readers can follow and understand easily what the writers try to convey. It means that with sequential words, readers can grasp some of the logical connection of the reading. They usually indicate the order of time or logical sequence, sometimes, but not always, having more importance in the order. Here are some sequential words or phrases.

- Indicating the order of objects
  Firstly, at first, secondly, next, lastly, finally, etc.

VII. Vocabulary in Context

1. Fill in the blank with the **boldfaced** word or phrase from the reading that best completes each sentence. Change the form of the word if necessary.
   (1) The chef, donning his white jacket, is proud of Godiva's trade secret fermentation process that adds _________ taste and flavor.
   (2) It is really _________ to understand a voluminous book in just 40 minutes through a YouTube post.
   (3) From the opening sequence, it is designed to _________ and captivate parents and kids alike.

2. Choose the word or phrase that best completes each sentence.
   (1) The moon _________ on the pond's surface.
   a. expanded b. enchanted c. shimmered d. discolored
   (2) He built a reputation as a(n) _________ preacher who could frame classical theology in ways that engaged people both inside and outside the church.
   a. spellbinding b. coward c. intelligent d fraudulent
   (3) The boat _________ the coast and looked for illegal smugglers.
   a. skirted b. escaped c. floated d. sailed

VIII. Grammar Point

Sentences starting with *Not only* (*Not, Never*) will make an inversion. That means the subject and the verb form of the sentence are changed in order and form, depending on the tense and number.

Not only do they function as a port, they also draw millions of tourists into their beautiful ports.

For example:
Not a single word did he say = He did not say a single word.
Not only did I go there, I saw it in my eyes.

IX. Writing a Summary

A summary is a short paragraph that provides the most important information from a reading. It usually includes the main ideas, not details. When you write a summary, don't copy from the reading. Use your own words.

Write a summary of the passage. It should not be more than five sentences. The first two sentences of the summary are below. Write two or three more sentences to complete the summary.

There are many beautiful ports in the world. They have their own unique characteristics and attract tourists and visitors from all over the world.

X. Topics for Discussion and Writing

1. When is the best time to visit Sydney in the southern hemisphere?

2. What is the most exciting activity you want to do when you visit each beautiful port introduced in the reading?

Did You Know?

Santorini, or Thira, is the top destination among the most romantic destinations in the Greek islands and also in the world. Santorini island is the site of one of the largest volcanic eruptions in the world and what remains today is a submerged volcano and a caldera. Apart from the fabulous caldera villages, Santorini is also famous for the romantic sunset, the volcano, and the luxurious resorts.

Readings in Ocean Topics

Unit 4

Whales around the Seas of Korea

I. Pre-reading

1. How are whales different from fish?
2. What is Moby Dick?
3. Where in Korea can you watch whales?

II. Vocabulary Preview

The following words appear in **bold** in the reading. Match each with its correct definition.

1. abound with	a. a legal agreement
2. captive	b. to be carried by the wind or water
3. contract	c. best, most desirable or favorable
4. drift	d. a suspension of activity
5. optimum	e. confined or imprisoned
6. moratorium	f. to have a lot of something
7. petroglyphs	g. carving or drawing on a rock made by prehistoric people

Whales around the Seas of Korea

Jangsaengpo Whale Museum (출처: 한국관광공사)

Have you heard the news that Jedori, a dolphin that had been illegally captured and kept at a zoo as a show animal for four years, was finally released to his home ground, the sea south of Jeju Island? Or have you been to Jangsaengpo Whale Museum which shows over a 100-year history of whaling industry in Korea? Or have you visited the Bangudae Petroglyphs to see the prehistoric engravings of whales? These questions naturally lead you to wonder how long humans on the Korean peninsula had been related to whales and where around Korea whales live. This writing will answer these questions you have.

Whaling in Korea can be traced back to prehistoric times. The **engravings** at the Bangudae Rock serve as the evidence to the fact that the Neolithic people living in the southeastern part of Korea were familiar with whaling. The scholars who discovered the **petroglyphs** in the early 1970s were amazed at the figures carved on the big vertical rock above the river. They included human beings, animals, and geometric symbols. While land animals such as deer and tigers number 46, diverse figures of whales take up 53 out of a total of 169 engraved animals. Experts identified several species of whales, a baby whale with its mother, and people on a boat dragging the hunted whale. These petroglyphs are presumably the oldest remains in the world that depict whales and whaling. It is believed that the ancient people tried to pass on the knowhow of hunting to the younger generation as well as wished good result in hunting when they engraved the objects of hunting.

In fact, the East Sea was known to **abound with** whales. *Samgukyusa*

Whale Watching (https://iwc.int/photo-gallery)

(the Heritage of the Three States) records the legend of Yeonorang and Seonyo of Silla. The couple lived in a village by the sea in present day Pohang. When they were collecting the seaweed on a seaside rock, the rock began to move and they were carried over the sea to Japan. The legend has it that they became the king and queen of Japan. Many people think the rock was actually a whale. But it is still hard to prove humans can ride a whale such a long distance from Korea to Japan. However, the legend suggests there must have been a lot of whales living in the East Sea.

In 1852, the South America, an American whaling ship, was **drifted** ashore to Yongdangpo, Busan. Even though this incident was the first encounter between Americans and Koreans, there was no verbal communication between them. Three years later in 1855 four American sailors, who said they were drifted from the **shipwreck**, landed on the shore of north Gangwon province. It was found they were the crew members of a U.S. whaler, Two Brothers. The truth was that they escaped the ship out of the excessive, tiring labor imposed on them. When these sailors were sent to China, the court ruled they go back to the whaling ship to fulfill their **contracts**. Whaling ships in the 19th century usually hunted sperm whales, whose oil was used to light the lamps at home and lubricate machines before being replaced by petroleum. The East Sea and the Pacific were the whaling ground of sperm whales as we see in Herman Melville's epic novel *Moby-Dick*. In fact many European whaling ships frequented the East Sea. Even Dok-do was named "Liancourt Rocks" after the French whaler, which 'discovered' the islets.

Jangsaengpo in Ulsan used to be the **base** of modern whaling due to its **optimum** location close to the route of whale migration. **Commercial** whaling in Korea, started by the Russians in the late 19th century, prospered during the period of Japanese **occupation** of Korea, and continued through 1986 when IWC(International Whale Commission) prohibited commercial whaling worldwide. The '**moratorium**' transformed the thriving town of the 1960s and 1970s to a ghost town. However, Jangsaengpo revived as a hot place where tourists can reminisce about the past memories with the whale museum and the whale watching tour instead of killing whales.

Many populations of whales were hunted in the 19th and 20th centuries and some are at risk of extinction. The **cetaceans** inhabiting the seas of Korea have faced the same fate. As many as 1,000 porpoises are caught in the fishing net in the Yellow Sea every year, and out of 55 incidentally caught minke whales in 2014, 54 were caught in Korea. Environmental activists such as Hotpinkdolphins complain Korea has a strange system in which whaling is illegal, but to sell whale meat from the bycatch is allowed. They also argue the illegal catching of whales disguised as bycatch must be stopped right away. Many things need to be done for the endangered sea mammals: The **captive** dolphins in aquariums should be returned to nature. The habitats of bottle-nosed dolphins around Jeju Island should be protected from the threatening noises from the wind turbines.

IV. Fact Check

Read the passage again and then read the following statements. Write a T if the statement is true and an F if false. If false, rewrite it to make it true.

1. _____ Jangsaengpo Whale Museum mainly displays artifacts found at Bangudae.

2. _____ The rock carvings at Bangudae show the scenes of hunting.

3. _____ The legend of Yeonorang and Seonyo has been handed down in Ulsan.

4. _____ In 1855 an American whaler landed at Gangwon Province to get water.

5. _____ Dokdo was named 'Liancourt Rocks' after an American whaling ship.

V. Reading Comprehension

Choose the best answer for each question.

1. What is the purpose of introducing the Bangudae Petroglyphs in the reading?
   a. To show the oldest artifacts related to whaling
   b. To demonstrate that Korea has a long history of whaling
   c. To explain the ancient people's religious system
   d. To compare the animals of the past and those of the present

2. Which statement is true about the legend of Yeonorang and Seonyo described in *Samgukyusa*?
   a. It concerns how Japan was founded by the couple.
   b. We can infer the couple were aristocrats.
   c. A whale carried the couple to Japan on its back.
   d. There must have been lots of whales in the East Sea.

3. What is the main idea of Paragraph 4?
   a. Many American whaling ships were drifted to Korea in the 19th century.
   b. A French whaling ship discovered Dok-do for the first time.
   c. Oil from sperm whale was used for lamps and machines.
   d. Many western whalers came to the East Sea to catch whales.

4. Which activity is NOT what environmental activists would do?
   a. They oppose to selling and eating whale meat.
   b. They comply with the decision to build wind power plants in Jeju Island.
   c. They demand whales and dolphins be released from zoos and aquariums.
   d. They warn against any activity harmful to whales.

5. Which of the following facts is NOT mentioned in the passage?
   a. The number of land animals carved at the Bangudae Petroglyphs.
   b. The kinds of whales engraved at the Bangudae Petroglyphs.
   c. The treatment of the drifters from the American whaler.
   d. The number of minke whales caught in 2014 around the world.

VI. Developing Reading Skills

Skimming vs. Scanning

Sometimes you don't have to read the whole text. Instead, you often need to read the text quickly to obtain certain information. You can use the technique of **skimming**, which means reading quickly, for main ideas. For skimming, read the entire first paragraph, then the first sentence of the following paragraphs, and finally the entire last paragraph. Skimming can be a good way to review the text you already read.

On the other hand, **scanning** is used to quickly find a fact or specific information. When you scan, think of what you are looking for, move your eyes quickly over the text, and then record the information.

You skim for the general idea, while you scan for a particular, detailed information.

VII. Vocabulary in Context

1. Fill in the blank with the **boldfaced** word or phrase from the reading that best completes each sentence. Change the form of the word if necessary.
   (1) On the seafloor south of Newfoundland, Canada, there lies the world's most famous __________, that of the Titanic.
   (2) The __________ are sea mammals including whales, dolphins, and porpoises.
   (3) T*he Diary of Anne Frank* was written by a Jewish girl during the Nazi __________ of the Netherlands.

2. Choose a word or phrase that best completes each sentence.
   (1) The company has its ________ in Seoul.
   a. base b. basis c. basic d. baser
   (2) Experts predict that space travel will be ________________ in the near future.
   a. commerce b. commercial
   c. commercialize d. commercialized
   (3) He had his initials __________ on the back of the watch.
   a. engrave b. engraving c. engraved d. to engrave

VIII. Grammar Point

In English, words inflect their forms in accordance with the context of a sentence, such as tense and subject-verb agreement. Modern English is said to be a weakly inflected language, having lost an extensive case system of Old English; Nouns have only traces of inflection in the form of plurals (*-(e)s*) and possessive, and pronouns are inflected.

Part of speech	Nominative case	Possessive case	Objective case
noun	ocean	ocean's	ocean
pronoun	he	his	him

Adjectives are inflected to indicate the comparative and the superlative, mostly adding -er or -est. On the other hand, conjugation refers to the inflection of verbs. Regular verbs form their past tense and past participle with the ending -(e)d as shown in *live—lived—lived* or *look—looked—looked*. However, there are irregular verbs which do not follow the conjugation rules but have unique conjugation patterns.

Complete the table by writing the past form and the past participle form of each verb below.

	past	past participle
grow		
ride		
show		

IX. Writing a Summary

A summary is a short paragraph that provides the most important information from a reading. It usually includes the main ideas, not details. When you write a summary, don't copy from the reading. Use your own words.

Write a summary of the passage. It should not be more than five sentences. The first two sentences of the summary are below. Write two or three more sentences to complete the summary.

Whales in the seas around Korea have left diverse traces on the lives of the Korean people. Whales appear in the prehistoric remains at Bangudae, and a history records a legend which suggests their presence in the East Sea.

____

____

____

____

X. Topics for Discussion and Writing

1. Why do you think whales should be protected in spite of the long history of whaling?

2. Do you think the small-scale coastal whaling should be preserved or stopped? Take the example of Taiji, Japan as shown in "Did You Know" section below.

Did You Know?

In July 1, 2019, Japan resumed commercial whale hunting in more than 30 years. In December 2018, the Japanese government announced that Japan would withdraw from the IWC to resume commercial whaling. In addition to this, Tokyo decided to give up Antarctic whaling that had been allowed in the name of scientific research in exchange for coastal commercial whaling. Japan has been accused of bending the rules. While whalers provided some parts to researchers, they sold the remaining meat for human consumption. Now ecologists are worried Japan's decision will eventually endanger the J-Stock, a small population of minke whales whose home is the seas of Japan, and the sei whales. Another concern is that Japan's withdrawal from the IWC could tempt other countries like South Korea, China, and Russia to resume commercial whaling. On the other hand, Taiji, a small Japanese whaling town, has drawn international criticism for its annual dolphin hunts. Against the demand that dolphin hunts must be stopped, Japanese government maintained its ground on preserving the country's whaling practice as a part of traditional culture.

Readings in Ocean Topics

Ocean Life

Unit 5

I. Pre-reading

1. Look at the photo of the mammals above. Can you identify what it is?
2. Do you know what makes a marine mammal a marine mammal? List some characteristics of marine mammals and then compare your answers with your classmates' answers.

Marine mammals	
kinds	
origin	
breathing	
other	

II. Vocabulary Preview

The following words appear in **bold** in the reading. Match each with its correct definition.

1. entirety	a. the fat of sea mammals
2. absorb	b. to take in or soak up something by chemical or physical action
3. lean time	c. a substance which does not readily allow the passage of heat or sound
4. blubber	d. the whole of something

5. insulator — e. a period of time when there isn't much food and one barely has enough to eat
6. bladder — f. to a great extent
7. immensely — g. anything inflated and hollow

III. Reading

Marine versus Land Mammals

Living on land versus living in the ocean involves a lot more than simply being wet. Differences in the way we deal with simple things, such as keeping our bodies warm, finding food to eat, sleeping, and moving require very different solutions.

Environmental differences and their impact on the creatures

Gravity/Weight: The effect of gravity on things on land is much greater than those in water. On land, our bodies must be able to support the **entirety** of their own weight. This is not true of animals that live in the ocean. In water, the weight of the body is supported by the water. As such, marine mammals need fewer bones and can grow much larger without suffering any negative effects. For example, whales are known to be evolved from a group of hoofed terrestrial animals like hippopotamuses, yet they are mostly bigger than those on land.

Temperature: On land, the temperature of the air can change fairly quickly. On sunny days, the weather can be quite warm, but get much cooler after dark. The temperature of the ocean changes much slower and remains fairly constant both day and night. In addition, mammals need to deal with the fact that water can **absorb** body heat many times faster than air can.

Pressure/Density: Water and air both have weight, which is something that most of us do not think about. Obviously water weighs more, and is **denser**, than air. For this reason, your weight is one-third lighter in water. Lost weight is equal to the water weight. Water weight (which is referred to as water **pressure**) and density must be dealt with by animals living in the sea.

Salinity/Salt: The ocean is full of salty water although the amount of **salinity** varies from area to area. Land mammals need fresh (un-salty) water to drink if they wish to stay alive. Marine mammals have had to adapt to a world where fresh water is not available, even though they need fresh water every bit as much as land animals.

Fat

Fat in most land animals including humans is generally not advantageous as it makes moving difficult because it is heavy. While some is necessary as an emergency **storage** of energy for use in case of **lean times**, it is generally not considered a benefit; hence most land mammals have relatively little body fat. Marine mammals, on the other hand, have a relatively large amount of body fat, which is called "**blubber**" and is beneficial for a number of different reasons.

First of all, fat is a good **insulator** in water. Land mammals have hair to keep themselves warm since hair has the ability to trap air against the skin, which is then heated, thus keeping the animal warm. It works well so long as it stays dry. When hair gets wet, it loses its ability to trap air, and loses its ability to keep the skin insulated. This is why we get cold when we are wet. Conversely, fat is a poor conductor of heat, meaning that fat traps heat, functioning like Styrofoam in a cooler box. Heat does not move through fat very well.

Secondly, fat floats. In the water, all animals need some way of floating. Fish typically have an organ called a "swim **bladder**" which is a gas-filled sac that helps them float, but mammals do not have anything like that. To help them float, marine mammals use their fat. Since marine animals breathe air through lungs and need to be on the surface of the water to breathe, being able to float is important.

Size and weight

As many know, dolphins are relatively small, but some whale species can get to be **immensely** large. The Blue Whale, the largest animal that has ever lived, can grow to be 30 meters long, about as tall as a 10-story building, and weigh up to 180 metric tons. They can grow this large because the ocean water supports their body weight easily and their skeletons do not have to support the weight as our skeleton does. Of course, they do not grow unlimitedly. Recent studies have found that marine mammal size is bound by the need to retain body heat as well as difficulties to acquire enough food to survive.

Food and water

Like us, marine mammals need both food and water to be alive. And like us, they cannot drink sea water because it has too much salt in it. Drinking sea water would kill both humans and dolphins alike. We obtain our drinking water from lakes and rivers. Then where do dolphins get their water from? They gain it through their food, mostly the fish they eat. Most marine mammals eat fish and get fresh water from them.

Creatures in the ocean seem to be very different from those on land in many aspects, the differences being mostly made by their living environments.

IV. Fact Check

Read the passage again and then read the following statements. Write a T if the statement is true and an F if false. If false, rewrite it to make it true.

1. _____ Gravity is one of the factors that affects the size and weight of mammals.

2. _____ Fat can be a benefit when there is not enough food.

3. _____ All creatures in water have a swim bladder to float.

4. _____ Marine mammals can grow as large as their skeletons can support.

5. _____ Mammals in water breathe the air, eat food, and drink fresh water.

V. Reading Comprehension

Choose the best answer for each question.

1. Compared to on land, temperature in the ocean __________.
   a. is warmer
   b. is colder
   c. changes more
   d. changes less

2. Marine mammals get fresh water from __________.
   a. rain b. runoff c. fish d. seaweed

3. Why can marine mammals be larger than land mammals?
   a. Due to the warmer temperature of the ocean
   b. Due to rich food
   c. Due to the less effect of gravity
   d. Due to larger skeletons

4. What is NOT true?
   a. Marine mammals have more fat than land mammals.
   b. Land mammals need stronger skeletons than marine mammals.
   c. Mammals need to maintain relatively high internal body temperatures.
   d. Ocean water is less dense than the air.

5. What is the main idea of the passage?
   a. Marine and land mammals have evolved adjusting to the environment they live in.
   b. Marine mammals and land mammals live in different environments.
   c. The environments where marine mammals and land mammals live are dissimilar.
   d. Marine mammals are much larger than land mammals.

VI. Developing Reading Skills

Read the passage again. Then complete the following outline.
What are some biggest differences between marine and land mammals?

1. Fat
   a. Marine mammals ______________________________
   ____
   b. Land mammals ______________________________
   ____

2. Size and weight
   a. Marine mammals ______________________________
   ____
   b. Land mammals ______________________________
   ____

3. Food and water
   a. Marine mammals ______________________________
   ____
   b. Land mammals ______________________________
   ____

VII. Vocabulary in Context

1. Fill in the blank with the **boldfaced** word or phrase from the reading that best completes each sentence. Change the form of the word if necessary.

(1) Fat from marine mammals is called __________.

(2) A(n) __________ helps to keep you cool or warm.

(3) Land mammals use fat just for energy __________.

2. Choose the word that best completes each sentence.

(1) Deeper under water, you feel more __________.

a. pressure b. saltiness c. weight d. warmth

(2) Something with less __________ than water will float.

a. salinity b. pressure c. gravity d. density

(3) __________ along with temperature affects the density of seawater.

a. Water pressure b. Salinity
c. Rain d. Gravity

VIII. Grammar Point

Passive voice

The passive voice is used to show interest in the person or object that experiences an action rather than the person or object that performs the action. Thus the subject and the object in active voice are reversed in passive voice as seen in the example below:

Active voice:

Humans have explored less than five percent of the ocean.

Passive voice:

Less than five percent of the ocean has been explored by humans.

IX. Writing a Summary

A summary is a short paragraph that provides the most important information from a reading. It usually includes the main ideas, not details. When you write a summary, don't copy from the reading. Use your own words.

Write a summary of the passage. It should not be more than five sentences. The first two sentences of the summary are below. Write two or three more sentences to complete the summary.

Different environments, like on land and in water, require different kinds of adjustment to the creatures who live there.

X. Topics for Discussion and Writing

1. Besides they are warm-blooded, what characteristics do you think mammals have, which distinguishes them from other sea life?

2. Think about marine mammals that you know. What kinds of similarities and differences do they have? How do those differences help them in their living?

Did You Know?

All mammals have hair including marine mammals. For polar bears, some seals, and sea lions, the hair acts as insulation to keep them warm. Other marine mammals, like whales and dolphins have hair only on their faces or lose their hair after they are born.

Readings in Ocean Topics

Aquaculture as an Alternative Way of Our Well-being

Unit 6

I. Pre-reading

1. Have you been to a nearby fish farm? What type of marine species did you see being grown there?
2. What do you think are the main reasons that more fishermen nowadays switch over to aquaculture instead of wild fishing?
3. Have you heard of IMTA (Integrated Multi-Trophic Aquaculture)? What do you think is the difference between it and other types of aquaculture?

II. Vocabulary Preview

The following words appear in **bold** in the reading. Match each with its correct definition.

1. pen	a. a crab, lobster, or shrimp
2. mollusk	b. seaweed and other marine plants
3. crustacean	c. the variety of life forms in a particular habitat or ecosystem
4. alga (pl. algae)	d. substances that help plants and animals to grow
5. nutrients	e. an animal which has a soft body and no backbone
6. biodiversity	f. a small area with a fence round it

III. Reading

Aquaculture as an Alternative Way of Our Well-being

Currently about a half of all seafood for human consumption comes from aquaculture. In ten years, it will be more than 60 percent. Aquaculture is the controlled process of **cultivating** aquatic species including fish and plants in aquatic environments like the coastal sea waters, fresh water lakes and rivers, and even on land in tanks. It serves different purposes such as food production, restoration of **endangered** marine species, wild fish population enhancement, and their habitat restoration.

There are four common types of aquaculture: mariculture, fish farming, algaculture, and integrated multitrophic aquaculture. Mariculture uses sea water. It can either be done next to an ocean, with a partitioned part of the ocean or in **pens** away from the ocean. The organisms raised in mariculture range from **mollusks** to sea food options like **crustaceans** and shellfish. Fish farming is the most common type of aquaculture done in fresh water or sea water. It is a way of selectively breeding fish for human consumption. Fish farming that provides a cheap source of protein is easier to manage than livestock farming; Fish are less care-intensive, only requiring food and proper water and temperature conditions. The process is also much less land-intensive as the size of pens needed to rear some fish such as trout is much smaller than the land space necessary for producing the same amount of protein from beef cattle. Algaculture involves the cultivation of **algae**. Algae are unique organisms that share animal and plant characteristics in that they are motile sometimes like other microbes but they also contain chloroplasts that make them green and allow them to photosynthesize like green plants. For economic feasibility, they have to be grown and harvested in large quantities. Integrated multi-trophic aquaculture (IMTA) is an efficient system of aquaculture where various species are mixed into a system to provide different nutritional needs for one another, thereby simulating various ecological systems that exist in the natural habitats. The IMTA makes use of the inter-species nutritional transfer to ensure maximum resource utilization by using the waste of larger organisms as food sources for the smaller ones. The system enables the **nutrients** to be recycled, meaning the practice is less wasteful and produces more products.

Aquaculture provides health benefits. Fish and other seafood are good sources of protein. They have strong nutritional elements like natural oils such as omega 3 fatty acid that can be directly added into our diet. Also since it offers white meat, it is better for the blood in reducing cholesterol levels as opposed to the red meat of livestock.

There can be economic benefits of aquaculture. Algae are being developed into alternative fuel sources that can replace the **contemporary** fossil fuels. Such attempts, if successful, could not only ease the dependency of the world on drilled fossil fuels but also reduce the price of energy by having it farmed. A farmable source of energy means that it can **revolutionize** the energy sector and create a more stable economy that avoids the **volatile** nature of petroleum business and replaces it with a more abundant and **inexhaustible** fuel source. Aquaculture can also increase the number of possible jobs in the market. It saves fishermen a lot of time because they do not have to spend days and nights on wild sea fishing. This enables them to have more free time to pursue other economic activities and engage in alternative businesses as extra sources of income. The incentive of less labor for more profits pushes wild fishers to switch over to fish farming and allows them to make more gains than before. Aquaculture can also reduce seafood trade deficit. Nations not adjacent to the sea depend on import for seafood, which **results in** a trade deficit on those nations. Aquaculture would reduce this deficit as low-cost local productions would provide fresher and cheaper seafood with **incurring** less import and transport costs.

Aquaculture **emits** lower greenhouse gas than livestock farming, and thus has environmental benefits. Algae produce fatty matter that can be harvested and used as an alternative fuel source, the only **by-products** of which, when burnt, would be cleaner and pollution-free water-like substance. Mollusks and seaweed function as a kind of buffer that protects the sea against the land-based pollutants. Aquaculture can also **obviate** the need for excessive wild fishing. A number of fish species are in danger of being **depleted** due to overfishing. Aquaculture provides an alternative by allowing fish farmers to breed those same species in captivity and to enable the wild fish populations to be **replenished**, preserving the marine ecosystem and **biodiversity**.

The primary responsibility of aquaculture is to efficiently complement wild-caught fish options to increase the amount of seafood available worldwide. The oceans cannot naturally provide the demand for seafood. Aquaculture is the valuable means to fill in the gap of supply and is a solution to providing future generations with healthy and environmentally friendly food options. With an estimated 10 billion people anticipated to **inhabit** the earth by 2050, the demand for animal protein will increase by way more than 50 percent. In order to stably feed the world's growing population with a healthy, lean protein, aquaculture's role is of the utmost importance. Aquaculture has the potential to improve the health of our planet and the health of our population.

IV. Fact Check

Read the passage again and then read the following statements. Write a T if the statement is true and an F if false. If false, rewrite it to make it true.

1. _____ In ten years, about 50 percent of all seafood for human consumption will come from aquaculture.

2. _____ Algae have plant characteristics in that they contain chloroplasts that allow them to photosynthesize.

3. _____ The red meat of livestock is better than the white meat of fish in reducing cholesterol levels in the blood.

4. _____ Nations not adjacent to the ocean will have more seafood trade deficit than the sea-adjacent nations.

5. _____ The primary function of aquaculture is to develop the method of wild fishing to increase the amount of seafood available worldwide.

V. Reading Comprehension

Choose the best answer for each question.

1. **What could be another title for the reading?**
   a. Four main types of aquaculture
   b. Health and economic benefits of aquaculture
   c. Environmental benefits of aquaculture
   d. The various ways in which aquaculture can benefit us

2. **Which statement about the four common types of aquaculture is NOT true?**
   a. Various species such as octopuses, lobsters, and clams are grown in mariculture.
   b. Fish farming can be carried out in either fresh water or sea water.
   c. Squids and shellfish are bred and reared in algaculture.
   d. IMTA is an attempt to emulate marine eco-systems that exist in the natural habitats.

3. **Which statement about the economic benefits of aquaculture is true?**
   a. The development of algae into alternative fuel sources is already successful.
   b. Aquaculture is less time-consuming than wild fishing.
   c. The disadvantage of more labor for less profits pushes fishermen to stick to wild sea fishing.
   d. Seeking seafood resources through aquaculture costs more than importing them.

4. **Which of the following phrases does NOT characterize the environmental benefits of aquaculture?**
   a. greenhouse gas emission
   b. relatively pollution-free
   c. creating less pollutants
   d. protection of marine biodiversity

5. **Which of the following statements is true based on the contents of the reading?**
   a. Fish farming has nothing to do with wild fish population enhancement.
   b. Omega 3 fatty acid functions to increase cholesterol levels in our body.
   c. Livestock farming in general emits more greenhouse gas than the confectionery industries.
   d. Pursuing aquaculture is one of the important means of providing healthy proteins for the world's population.

VI. Developing Reading Skills

Using overall contents to create sub-headings:

A reading passage often does not have sub-headings. Sub-headings, if used, should be put right above paragraphs that introduce new ideas or topics with or without lengthy supporting details. Creating sub-headings based on overall contents can help readers better comprehend and remember the most crucial information from the passage.

The text consists of six paragraphs. One sub-heading may be followed by just a single paragraph, or more than two paragraphs may be bundled up under the same sub-heading. How many sub-headings do you think are necessary under the macro-title "Aquaculture as an Alternative Way of Our Well-being?" What are they and which paragraph should be put under which sub-heading? To determine what sub-headings to be used depends on each individual content-analysis. The following is a sample answer:

Aquaculture as an Alternative Way of Our Well-being
The Definition of Aquaculture and the Purposes behind It
Paragraph One
Four Common Types of Aquaculture
Paragraph Two
The Health Benefits of Aquaculture
Paragraph Three
The Economic Benefits of Aquaculture
Paragraph Four
The Environmental Benefits of Aquaculture
Paragraph Five
The Primary Function of Aquaculture and Conclusion
Paragraph Six

Now read the text again with the above outline in mind, and then see, with your eyes off the text, how much crucial information you can remember. Do the sub-headings help? If yes, then why? If no, why not?

VII. Vocabulary in Context

1. Fill in the blank with the **boldfaced** word or phrase from the reading that best completes each sentence. Change the form of the word if necessary.

(1) 14% of primate species are highly ______________.

(2) The musicians' studies are devoted almost entirely to ______________ music genres such as Hip-Hop, Reggae, Rap, and Rock'n' Roll.

(3) One's failure to comply with the COVID-19 quarantine rules will ______ prosecution by the public health authorities.

2. Choose a word or phrase that best completes each sentence.

(1) The region has a(n) ______________ deposit of iron ore.

a. volatile b. inexhaustible c. revolutionized d. healthy

(2) This new evidence _______ the need for any further enquiries into the defendant's case.

a. emits b. incurs c. restores d. obviates

(3) Our body needs rest to _____ its powers to protect us from viruses and bacteria.

a. replenish b. deplete c. inhabit d. cultivate

VIII. Grammar Point

Five Types of Relative Clauses

Type 1 Relative Clause Pronouns used as the Subject: This is the case where the antecedent noun (phrase) functions as the subject of relative clause if inserted inside the clause.

For example:
I thanked *the woman who helped me.*

Algae contain *chloroplasts which allow them to photosynthesize like green plants.*

Type 2 Relative Clause Pronouns used as the Object of a Verb: This is the case where the antecedent noun (phrase) functions as the object of relative clause if inserted inside the clause.

For example:
The man who(m) I saw was Mr. Jones.

The natural oils from fish which we add into our diet reduce the cholesterol levels in the blood.

Type 3 Relative Clause Pronouns used as the Object of a Preposition: This is the case where the antecedent noun (phrase) functions as the object of a preposition inside the relative clause.

For example:
She is *the woman who(m) I told you about.*

The protein deficiency problem which African children are faced with can be overcome by helping the NGOs to establish local fish farming facilities.

Type 4 Relative Clause Pronoun used as the Possessor of a Noun: This is the case where the antecedent noun (phrase) functions as the possessor of a noun inside the relative clause.

For example:
I know *the man whose bicycle was stolen*.

Algae's fatty matter can be used as *an alternative fuel source the only by-products of which, when burnt, would be cleaner and pollution-free water-like substance*.

Type 5 Relative Clause Pronouns used as the Connecting Conjunction: This is the case where the relative pronoun functions as the modifying connector between the preceding sentence and the following relative clause.

For example:
Tom failed in the exam, which shocked everyone in the class.

Nations not adjacent to the sea depend on import for seafood, which results in a trade deficit on those nations.

IX. Writing a Summary

A summary is a short text that provides the most important information from a reading. It usually includes the main ideas, not details. When you write a summary, don't copy from the reading. Use your own words.

Write a summary of the reading. It should not be more than twelve sentences, given the length of the reading in this unit. The first two sentences of the summary are below. Write ten more sentences to complete the summary.

Aquaculture is the process of cultivating marine species in controlled aquatic environments. Mariculture, fish farming, algaculture, and IMTA are four common types of aquaculture.

X. Topics for Discussion and Writing

1. Can you think of additional benefits of aquaculture not mentioned in the reading? Do you think there could be some disadvantages or even negative aspects of aquaculture? If yes, what would they be?

2. Write a short essay on how the food shortage problem in Africa can be overcome.

Did You Know?

The world's fish farming technologies are currently progressing in such a remarkable way that now there is almost no species that cannot be farmed, including hard-to-tame tuna. Out of all tuna species, Bluefin tuna, one of the world's most endangered and most valuable fish species, has become a hot topic of research for aquaculture scientists whose aim is to develop a farming method to breed and grow them within the next five years. They are not well-suitable for aquaculture, for the quick-tempered, ferocious, fastest swimmers would die on collision with the walls of narrow sea pens when swimming at that high speed, and often cannibalize one another when threatened.

Readings in Ocean Topics

The Dark Side of Technology

Unit 7

I. Pre-reading

1. Including canned tuna and dried anchovies, how often do you eat seafood?
2. What is your favorite and least favorite seafood?
3. How would you feel if you suddenly could not eat seafood anymore?

II. Vocabulary Preview

The following words appear in **bold** in the reading. Match each with its correct definition.

1. concerted	a. continuous change
2. flux	b. coordinated, working together
3. designate	c. of an animal that hunts and eating other animals
4. predatory	d. to assign to an official status
5. devastate	e. to replace
6. supplant	f. to destroy or ruin
7. spawn	g. to give rise to, to create (something new)

III. Reading

Overfishing

Your cell phone vibrates because your high school friend visiting the Philippines has posted a picture of the dinner she was about to eat. The large library near your childhood home now contains less information than you have in your pocket. The amount of information that once only libraries could contain now sits in our pocket. Worst of all, your mother knows exactly how much money you charged to her card and calls you before you have left the store. Detractors say that our lives are filled with trivial knowledge, our relationships superficial, and our ability to think **supplanted** by our ability to google. But technology has brought with it an even greater problem: it is destroying the planet.

Technological advancement has affected every field of human endeavour, and fishing is no exception. In the 1990s, great advancements were made involving radar that allowed fishing ships to vastly increase their yields. Originally touted as a great success **spawning** a new business model, this practice has ultimately become a **devastating** one. Fish have been captured and consumed at a rate faster than they can reproduce, giving rise to unsustainable fishing.

One out of every seven people around the world relies directly on fish for their survival, and throughout human history, there have always been enough fish for human consumption. Indeed, in English we often say, "There are always more fish in the ocean," an expression used not for fish but frequently for people—for example, when two people break up, the phrase is used to console them, reminding them that there are many other people in the world and they will soon find new partners. But the phrase in its literal interpretation is quickly becoming ironic.

We have all seen photos of fishers standing beside their latest catch, a strung-up fish larger than the humans who caught it. But these photos are frequently of older vintage; many of the larger species of **predatory** fish have been decimated if not completely exterminated. When large fish species are no longer available for fishing, humans target the next largest fish, and the once medium-sized fish now become the largest ones, a process known as 'fishing down.' Trophic levels, which denote a species' level in the food chain, are frequently being rewritten, and many ecosystems in the ocean are in a state of **flux** due to human consumption.

According to a recent SOFIA (State of World Fisheries and Aquaculture) report, 89.5% of our oceans are fully fished or overfished. Some 52% of the oceanic species we commonly eat are fully exploited, and while this is not a serious problem, it also means they are one step away from being overexploited. The species that are already overexploited account for 17%, while 7% of the species are fully **depleted**, with another 1% recovering. Only about 20% are classified as 'moderately exploited.'

Yet the problem remains invisible to most consumers; supermarkets and seafood restaurants continue to stock fish and other marine catches. When one area of the ocean is depleted, fisheries simply move to another part, wreaking havoc in more ecosystems. Some areas have been **designated** as 'no-take zones' or 'marine-protected areas.' However, only about 1% of our oceans is fully no-take, and another 1% allows fishing of certain, specified species. As is to be expected, such areas become officially **declared** 'no-take' only after the damage has already been done, to allow certain species to rebuild their numbers. It is, unfortunately, nearly impossible to enforce the law on the open ocean, and European-based super-**trawlers**[1] still receive EU funding even after being caught engaging in illegal fishing.

Another related problem with trawling methods is that they capture marine life indiscriminately. Literally billions of dolphins, sharks, marine turtles, and even corals, sea birds and fish that are not yet fully grown are caught in the nets and die each year because of our fishing methods. This is known as by-fishing.

Many in the scientific community believe that the damage can still be reversed but not without a lot of effort. General awareness of the issue needs to be raised. Existing laws will need to be enforced and new ones written. Illegal harvesting of the ocean remains the greatest threat to our marine food supply.

Consumers of fish and other seafood are encouraged to use the Seafood Guide produced by the Marine Conservation Society, available from www.fishonline.org and also as a smart phone app. Using a five-point rating system, the guide informs consumers of what fish may be safely eaten and which should be avoided. It also tells us how to read the labels on supermarket fish and what questions to ask restaurants regarding the fish on their menus. With a **concerted** effort from consumers, the ocean may be able to return to a state of sustainability.

---

1) **Trawling:** a method of fishing in which large nets are dragged by a boat. A super-trawler is a ship that captures tons of marine life every day.

IV. Fact Check

Read the passage again and then read the following statements. Write a T if the statement is true and an F if false. If false, rewrite it to make it true.

1. _____ We should be careful of what seafood we eat in order to help reverse overfishing

2. _____ Less than a quarter of our seafood is moderately exploited.

3. _____ 'Fishing down' means catching fish in deeper sections of the ocean.

4. _____ 'By-fishing' refers to catching fish illegally.

5. _____ Twenty percent of the ocean is protected.

V. Reading Comprehension

Choose the best answer for each question.

1. All of the following statements are true, but one was not mentioned in the article. Which one?
   a. 52% of fish we consume are fully exploited.
   b. 2% of the ocean is protected from overfishing to some extent.
   c. 90% of the ocean's main predators have been wiped out by overfishing.
   d. 20% of the species we consume are moderately exploited.

2. Which of the following statements is mentioned in the article about supertrawlers?
   a. They catch fish with nets.
   b. They catch marine life that cannot be sold as food.
   c. They can capture whales under the pretence of scientific research.
   d. Any trawler can receive EU funding.

3. Which of the following methods is NOT mentioned to reduce or reverse the effects of overfishing?
   a. Raising the public's awareness of the issue
   b. Enforcing existing laws
   c. Making new laws
   d. Internet campaigns

4. What is the main point of the final paragraph?
   a. To give information about www.fishonline.org
   b. To convey what consumers can do about overfishing
   c. To explain how to read the labels on supermarket fish
   d. To encourage consumers to ask questions to restaurant staff

5. How can illegal fishing in no-take zones be enforced?
   a. Increased use of police ships
   b. GPS tracking of super-trawlers
   c. Eliminate funding for ships and companies and catch those who ignore the law.
   d. The article doesn't say.

VI. Developing Reading Skills

The introduction of the main text details the development of technology while the main body enumerates the problems of overfishing. When we write conclusions to an essay or any text, we need to provide a sense of finality.

One strategy for this is to point towards the future, which is what the conclusion above does. It also shifts attention from the problem to the solutions. What are some of the solutions the concluding paragraphs suggest?

____

____

____

____

____

____

VII. Vocabulary in Context

1. Fill in the blank with the **boldfaced** word or phrase from the reading that best completes each sentence. Change the form of the word if necessary.

(1) When something changes all the time, it is in a state of ____________.

(2) If law-enforcers say something is wrong, then that activity has been ______________ illegal.

(3) Sharks are ______________ animals.

(4) If a company has no more money left, then its funds are ___________.

2. Choose a word or phrase that best completes each sentence.

(1) New ways of doing things often ______________ old traditions.

a. supplant b. designate c. flux d. concerted

(2) Although they survived the earthquake, their lives were ____________.

a. depleted b. flux c. devastated d. predatory

(3) Global warming can be reversed, but only with ______________ effort from all.

a. concerted b. fluxed c. predatory d. devastated

VIII. Grammar Point

Note the following sentence:

Existing laws will need to be enforced and new ones written.

This sentence contains two subjects: *existing laws* and *new ones*. However,
the verb of the second clause may look a little strange because *written* is not a complete verb. In this case, the second verb 'borrows' the modal verb of the first sentence; hence the actual meaning is *Existing laws will need to be enforced and new ones will be written*. When this borrowing occurs, no comma is placed between the two clauses even though a new subject is introduced.

IX. Writing a Summary

The reading text above contains nine paragraphs. Write a one-sentence summary for each paragraph.

1.

2.

3.

4.

5.

6.

7.

8.

9.

Now combine each of the sentences above into a paragraph.
Use transitions, pronouns, etc., for cohesion.

X. Topics for Discussion and Writing

1. In what ways is overfishing comparable to global warming?

2. How will human cultures be affected if overfishing is not reversed? How would it be different than today?

"Fins are for Sharks!" Poster
SEPTEMBER 15, 2013 BY SHARK

Did You Know?

Do you like sharks? Most people don't. However, the population of sharks has decreased by 90% around the world because of overfishing, and by 99% around America's east coast. This is largely due to the demand for shark fin soup.

How to Fly Underwater

Unit 8

I. Pre-reading

BC Jacket & Regulator System

Weight Leads

1. What is your favorite water sport? Why?
2. The above pictures show three pieces of diving equipment. Can you guess for what purposes they are used?
3. What safety measures do you think should be taken in scuba diving?

II. Vocabulary Preview

The following words appear in **bold** in the reading. Match each with its correct definition.

1. tender
2. propulsion
3. coral reefs
4. accumulate
5. weightless
6. buoyancy

a. ridges of colorful underwater subtances, the top of which is usually just below the surface of the sea
b. not affected by the earth's gravity
c. the power that moves something in a forward direction
d. the ability that something has to float on a liquid or in the air
e. a person on watch or an assistant
f. to increase in number or amount over a period of time

III. Reading

How to Fly Underwater

Diving allows sea lovers to enjoy the spectacular view of the underwater world. While experiencing an awesome sense of **weightlessness**, divers can watch a variety of **coral reefs** and a great number of sea creatures. Diving sports can be divided into three different activity types: snorkeling, skin diving, and **scuba**[1] diving. The first two activities are regarded by most people as the same sport because both sports use the same equipment and most of the time, are spent on the surface looking down at the world below, although skin divers can hold their breath and occasionally swim down to spend as much time underwater as possible to explore the sea bottom. On the other hand, scuba divers do not have to resurface for air, but carry air tanks on their back to breathe. Scuba diving requires at least the first-level Open Water Scuba Diver certification with lessons on fundamental diving skills and principles. The purpose of this article is to give information on some basics of diving activities, diving equipment, and crucial safety measures.

Scuba Tanks with BC jackets and Regulators attached

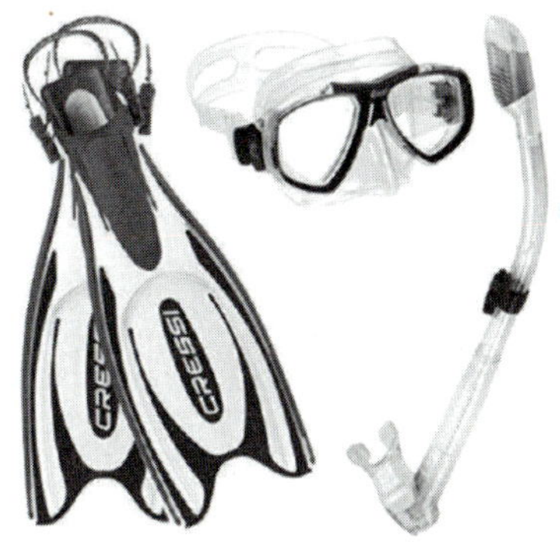

Fins, a diving mask, and a snorkel

Required pieces of equipment for snorkeling and skin diving are a diving mask, a snorkel, fins, and wet suits. A diving mask must have a nose pocket that enables the squeezing of your nose for **equalization**.[2] A snorkel lets you breathe while staying afloat. Scuba Tanks with BC jackets and Regulators attached Fins, a diving mask, and a snorkel Fins usually come with the use of rubber boots and assist divers' motion and **propulsion** under the water. Because the water temperature is lower than your body

1) **Scuba** is short for Self-Contained Underwater Breathing Apparatus and refers to the equipment used for underwater breathing.

2) **Equalization:** This is a term used in scuba diving that describes a safety practice taken when descending underwater. Read the last five sentences of the text for its meaning.

temperatureand during diving activities you may quickly lose body heat and suffer from **hypothermia**, it is recommended that wet suits be worn in all non-tropical weather zones.

For scuba activity, four more gadgets are required in addition to snorkeling and skin diving equipment: a **buoyancy** control (BC) jacket, a scuba tank, regulators, and lead weights. BC jackets control divers' buoyancy by inflating or deflating its internal rubber bladders. Scuba tanks are filled with compressed air and provide your source of breathing air. You breathe through a regulator that has a mouthpiece at its end and regulatesthe flow of air from the high-pressure air tank. Regulators come with air and depth gauges and also have a hose attached to the BC device for inflation. The regulator system has two additional hoses other than the one attached to the BC jacket: a black colored one and the other yellow colored with mouthpieces at the end of both. The first one is the primary regulator hose you will be breathing through. The other is a back-up hose used for **buddy breathing**.[3] With the head down below the surface, a diver's body, with an air tank on the back, has internal air spaces and will stay afloat. To **descend** under the water, lead weights must be used. A weight belt worn around a diver's waist or lead weights put directly into specially designed pockets of the BC jacket can be used.

Diving activities are exciting and fun, but there are accompanying dangers as well. Accident-causing surface and underwater situations can be prevented

---

3) **Buddy Breathing:** Due to safety concern, it is recommended that scuba diving always be done at least in a pair of two people. Buddy breathing refers to the act of sharing air with your diving partner in case she or he ran out of oris low on air in the scuba tank.

by using safety accessories and by obeying crucial diving rules. A dive knife attached to the leg or the BC jacket can be used when a diver gets **entangled** in fishermen's nets or underwater plants. A floating buoy (FB) is string-connected to a solid diving point under the water, and the FB is used to let a diver's presence known and to warn passing boats on the surface not to come near the buoy when the diver **ascends**. A whistle attached to the BC is used to get the attention of the surface **tenders** while boat diving. Its loud noise can be used to call for help in case of emergencies under the water. A water-resistant flashlight is required during nighttime diving. While providing a source of light underwater, it also marks the diver's presence on ascent. A wristband dive computer is worn to monitor one's bottom time, depth, and so on to prevent **decompression sickness**.[4] It **obviates** the need to manually calculate one's diving time-plan using the **Dive Table**.[5]

Decompression sickness occurs when a diver ascends too fast and the nitrogen **accumulated** in our body fails to be released out of the body with the suddenly decreasing water pressure. When we breathe on land, normally only oxygen is used from the air, and nitrogen and other gases are expelled out of our body system. In diving, however, due to water pressure, unused nitrogen is trapped and absorbed in our body tissues, and with increasing depths, our body accumulates proportionally more nitrogen. In fast ascension, bubbles are formed at the joints by the unreleased nitrogen, causing severe pain to a diver at the joints of arms and legs. So, when diving into deeper areas, for gradual release of nitrogen, you must make sure that your dive plan follows the Dive Table. Another important safety practice to be taken when going underwater is equalization. The water pressure increases by 1 atmosphere every 10 meters deep, and our body in general easily adapts to this increasing pressure except for the middle ear. To equalize the increasing pressure in the air space of the middle ear, divers squeeze and close their nose using fingers while trying to blow air out of the nasal cavity. The failure to properly equalize causes severe pain in the ear and can cause the eardrum to **rupture**. With all these necessary safety measures taken, diving activities can be accident-free and more enjoyable.

---

4) **Decompression Sickness:** An illness that occurs with too much nitrogen accumulated in one's body tissues

5) **Dive Table:** Prepared originally by the US Navy for a safety guideline for deep-sea diving, it specifies time intervals to be spent at specific depths when ascending to the surface.

IV. Fact Check

Read the passage again and then read the following statements. Write a T if the statement is true and an F if false. If false, rewrite it to make it true.

1. _____ The license of Open Water Scuba Diver is the most basic level of tank-diving certification you can get from a dive instructor.

2. _____ Skin divers carry air tanks on their back to breathe.

3. _____ A weight belt is the main diving accessory that controls divers' buoyancy.

4. _____ The deeper we go, the more oxygen our body accumulates.

5. _____ In all circumstances, divers must slowly ascend to the surface on finishing one's dive.

V. Reading Comprehension

Choose the best answer for each question.

1. What does the reading NOT mention?
   a. Three types of diving activities and their differences
   b. How to treat decompression sickness
   c. Safety equipment used for scuba diving
   d. Safety measures to be taken while scuba diving

2. What could be another title for the reading?
   a. The reasons why people enjoy scuba diving
   b. Dangers that accompany all diving activities
   c. Diving activities, necessary equipment, and safety measures
   d. Diving accessories used for snorkeling, skin diving, and scuba diving

3. Which statement is NOT true about scuba diving equipment?
   a. A BC jacket has internal rubber bladders for its inflation or deflation.
   b. A scuba tank, when fully charged, holds high air pressure.
   c. The regulator system consists of three hoses.
   d. Lead weights are used for both descent and ascent while diving.

4. Which of the following statements is true about the safety accessories for diving?
   a. A dive knife can be used as a weapon against a possible shark attack.
   b. Both the FB and the flashlight can enhance divers' safety while resurfacing.
   c. The whistle cannot be used while floating on the water surface.
   d. The Dive Table cannot be stored in a wristband dive computer.

5. Which of the following statements is NOT true about decompression sickness?
   a. It can be effectively treated when a proper amount of oxygen is accumulated in our body.
   b. It occurs as a result of an excessive amount of nitrogen accumulated in our body.
   c. It does not occur if you are a snorkeler.
   d. Fast ascension does not allow nitrogen to be properly released out of our body system.

VI. Developing Reading Skills

Classifying Information

Think about how the information and ideas are interrelated in the reading. Can you classify the ideas based on the overall contents? Readers will be able to better understand and recall the most crucial information of the reading passage by information classification.

Using a chart to classify information: Re-read the passage and classify the contents using the chart below.

<table>
<tr><th colspan="2">Classification</th><th>Contents</th></tr>
<tr><td colspan="2">Reasons that sea lovers like scuba diving</td><td></td></tr>
<tr><td rowspan="3">Three Diving Sports</td><td>Snorkeling</td><td></td></tr>
<tr><td>Skin Diving</td><td></td></tr>
<tr><td>Scuba Diving</td><td></td></tr>
<tr><td rowspan="2">Pieces of Equipment & Uses</td><td>Snorkeling & Skin Diving</td><td></td></tr>
<tr><td>Scuba Diving</td><td></td></tr>
<tr><td colspan="2">Safety Accessories & Uses</td><td></td></tr>
<tr><td rowspan="2">Safety Practices</td><td>Decompression Sickness</td><td></td></tr>
<tr><td>Equalization</td><td></td></tr>
</table>

Now read the text again with the above information classification in mind, and then see, with your eyes off the text, how much crucial contents you can recall. Is the chart helpful? If yes, then why? If no, why not?

VII. Vocabulary in Context

1. Fill in the blank with the **boldfaced** word or phrase from the reading that best completes each sentence. Change the form of the word if necessary.

(1) If one quickly lose body heat, he or she may die of ____________.

(2) If someone is ____________ in something such as a rope, wire, or net, he/she is caught in it very firmly.

(3) A peaceful solution would ____________ the need to send a UN military force.

2. Choose a word or phrase that best completes each sentence.

(1) To __________ is to go down and to __________ is to go up.

a. ascend, equalize
b. descend, propel
c. ascent, descent
d. descend, ascend

(2) Eggshells are very porous. Over time more and more air enters the shell, and the egg has ________ to float to the top in a bowl of water.

a. buoy b. buoying c. buoyancy d. buoyant

(3) The water pipe in our house __________ because of the cold.

a. ruptured b. compressed c. obviated d. accumulated

VIII. Grammar Point

Subjunctive Verbs: When sentences have matrix verbs the meanings of which stress importance or urgency of a proposition, subjunctive verbs (simple forms of verbs) are to be used in embedded clauses.

For example:

The US Navy **recommends** that all divers **do** a mandatory safety stop at 4.5 meters for 3 minutes while surfacing.
The professor **demands** that all the students **be** on time.
The employee **insisted** that his salary **increase** by 10 percent.
The tour guide **recommended** that we **not go** to the park at night.

IX. Writing a Summary

A summary is a short paragraph that provides the most important information from a reading. It usually includes the main ideas, not details. When you write a summary, don't copy from the reading. Use your own words.

Write a summary of the passage. It should not be more than five sentences. The first sentences of the summary are given below. Write two or three more sentences to complete the summary.

Two safety measures to be taken while scuba diving are slow ascension and equalization. One must follow the Dive Table to prevent decompression sickness.

____

____

____

X. Topics for Discussion and Writing

1. Discuss with a partner what additional safety measures other than those mentioned on the text you think should be taken while scuba diving.
2. Write a short essay about a dangerous situation you were in during a sporting event and how you overcame the situation.

Did You Know?

To treat decompression sickness, sometimes called 'nitrogen intoxication', the diver must be immediately taken to the nearest recompression chamber (The one closest to the Busan area is at the Naval Academy in Jinhae.) and be placed in a hyperbaric room. Then, the diver will be put to the same underwater pressure as he or she was actually in, and becomes cured as the accumulated nitrogen bubbles get released out of the body with a gradual decrease of the pressure.

Coral Reefs, Lifeblood of Marine Life

Unit 9

I. Pre-reading

1. Have you ever been snorkeling or seen coral reefs or underwater life? If so, when and where did you see them and how did you like them?
2. If not, would you like to see them? Why?
3. Do you know any place we can see coral reefs?

II. Vocabulary Preview

The following words appear in **bold** in the reading. Match each with its correct definition.

1. sweep	a. to move, especially quickly and powerfully
2. release	b. to keep alive
3. shallow	c. extremely and surprisingly good
4. extraordinary	d. to destroy the normal continuance or unity of something
5. wondrous	e. very unusual, special, unexpected, or strange
6. interrupt	f. having little depth
7. sustain	g. to allow a substance to flow out from somewhere

III. Reading

Coral Reefs, Lifeblood of Marine Life

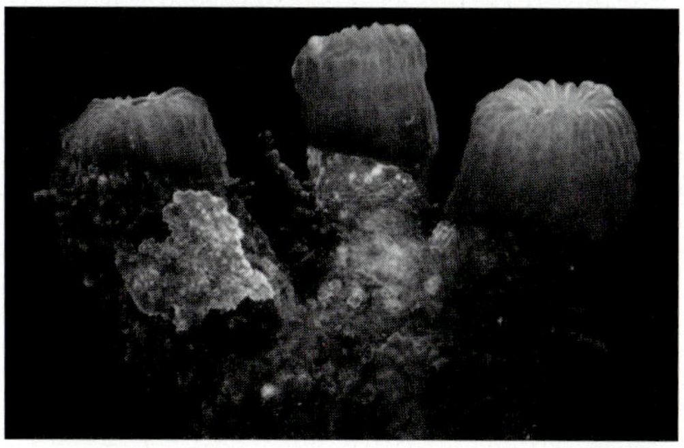

Coral reefs are biologically rich and economically valuable ecosystems that are essential to the marine life as well as humans. Are corals animals, plants, or rocks? Aristotle classified corals as 'zoophyta,' meaning plantanimals, animals that have characteristics of plants. However, most people believed them to be plants until British astronomer, William Herschel (1738 - 1822) found via microscope that corals had the thin skins of an animal, lacking the cell walls of plants.

Corals are tiny, soft-bodied organisms related to **sea anemones**[1] and jellyfish. An individual coral is known as a polyp, a very small and simple organism consisting mostly of a stomach and **tentacle**[2]-like arms that are used to capture its food from the water and **sweep** into its mouths.

Polyps attach their bodies together to build one large body, called a coral colony. These polyp colonies grow and die and endlessly repeat this cycle, slowly making stony corals that look like rocks. Most colonies are either entirely male or entirely female, and **release** eggs into the water to mate.

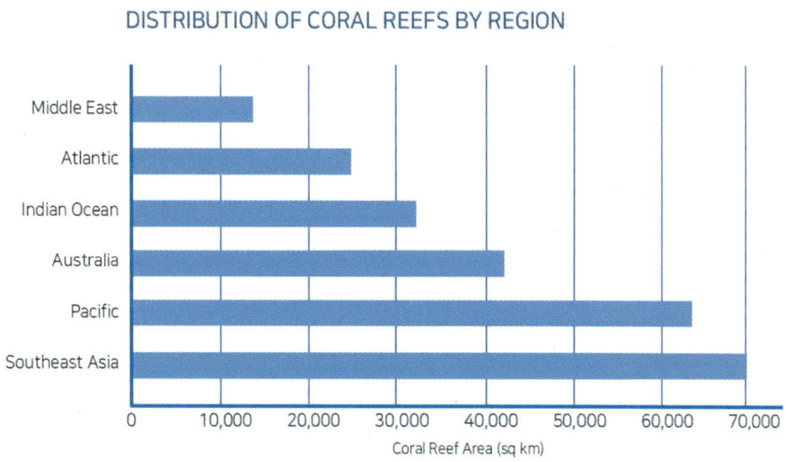

Source: The Economic Impact of Coral Reefs, March 20, 2015

1) **Sea anemone:** any of numerous usually solitary polyps whose form, bright and varied colors, and cluster of tentacles superficially resemble a flower
2) **Tentacle:** one of the long, thin parts like arms of some sea animals, used for feeling and holding things, and catching food, or moving

This results in microscopic, swimming coral **larvae** which attach to submerged rocks or other hard surfaces to clone themselves into a new, independent colony and eventually form a coral reef.

Coral reefs are usually found in **shallow** waters at a depth of less than 45 m although some extend up to about 135 m deep. They are found all around the world in tropical and **subtropical** oceans. In recent years, scientists have also discovered cold water coral reefs off the coast of Norway and deep underwater in the Mediterranean Sea.

Being limited mostly to shallow waters, perhaps surprising to some, the extent of coral reefs reaches less than 0.1% of the earth's surface, or 0.2% of the ocean's surface, McIntyre reported in 2010. Although they occupy very small areas, coral reefs offer homes to 25% of the entire marine life, which shows an **extraordinary** variety of marine species - fish, **algae** and microorganisms. Some scientists estimate the total diversity of life found in, on, and around all coral reefs up to 2 million species. After all, coral reefs are some of the most beautiful and biologically diverse habitats in the ocean.

Coral reefs are significant to people as well. The importance of coral reefs extends far beyond the pleasure they bring to the people who dive to see colorful fish, intricate formations, and **wondrous** sea creatures. They provide economic and environmental benefits to hundreds of millions of people. They are not only an important source of food, medicines, and tourism, but also a geological protector of shorelines and wetlands against erosion, property damage, and loss of life. Globally, half a billion people are estimated to live within 100 kilometers of a coral reef and benefit from its production and protection.

Despite their importance for humans as well as marine life, coral reefs are severely threatened today. In some places, reefs have been entirely destroyed, and in many places, they appear to be a pale shadow of what they once were, through a process known as **coral bleaching**[3]. The greatest threats to reefs globally are rising water temperatures and **acid**[4] seas linked to rising **carbon dioxide**[5] levels. High water temperatures and ocean acidification, which make it difficult for corals to build their calcium carbonate skeletons, kill coral colonies. Global warming has already increased levels of coral bleaching, and this is predicted to increase in severity in the coming years. According to the World Wide Fund (WWF),

---

3) **Coral bleaching:** a process where corals expel the algae living in their tissues causing the coral to turn completely white

4) **Acid:** any liquid substances that can react with and sometimes dissolve other materials with a pH less than 7.

5) **Carbon dioxide:** the gas formed when carbon is burned, or that people or animals breathe out

roughly one-quarter of coral reefs worldwide are already considered damaged beyond repair.

Local threats are equally severe. Destructive fishing practices such as dynamite fishing, and overfishing affect the ecological balance of coral reef communities, **interrupting** the food chain. Careless boating, diving, snorkeling, and fishing happen around the world, destroying coral reefs. Urban and industrial waste, **sewage**[6], **agrochemicals**[7], and oil dumped into water are poisoning them. Live coral is removed from reefs for economic benefits. All these human activities are greatly destroying priceless coral reefs.

Coral reefs are biologically rich and complex ecosystems that are essential not only to ocean health, but also to human health and well-being. However, today climate change, **pollution**, careless tourism, and overfishing are all causing harm, resulting in coral bleaching. **Dazzling** and life-**sustaining** organisms are disappearing. Imminent actions are required to reduce any threats to coral reefs. There are various ways we can help to protect the lifeblood of marine life, coral reefs. Our simple actions can help save them. A small action goes a long way!

---

6) **Sewage:** waste matter such as water or human urine
7) **Agrochemical:** a chemical used in agriculture

IV. Fact Check

Read the passage again and then read the following statements. Write a T if the statement is true and an F if false. If false, rewrite it to make it true.

1. _____ Aristotle classified corals as plants.

2. _____ Polyps form a colony by attaching their bodies together.

3. _____ Coral reefs live only in shallow waters.

4. _____ High water temperatures and ocean acidification are two of the biggest threats to coral reefs worldwide.

5. _____ Coral bleaching has slowed down in recent years.

V. Reading Comprehension

Choose the best answer for each question.

1. What are corals?
   a. plants
   b. animals
   c. rocks
   d. all the above

2. Coral reefs are NOT found in ____________ .
   a. shallow waters
   b. tropical and subtropical oceans
   c. off the coast of Norway and in the Mediterranean Sea
   d. the deep sea in the Pacific Ocean

3. Which human activity is NOT the cause of coral bleaching?
   a. Reducing pollution
   b. Touching corals
   c. Dumping sewage into water
   d. Overfishing

4. What is NOT true about coral reefs?
   a. Coral reefs extend 0.2% of the ocean's surface.
   b. Global threats to coral reefs are high water temperatures and overfishing.
   c. 25% of marine life lives in, on, and around coral reefs.
   d. Rising water temperatures have affected coral bleaching.

5. What is the main idea of the passage?
   a. Coral reefs are also found in cold water.
   b. Corals are plant-animals.
   c. Coral reefs should be protected for many reasons.
   d. Coral reefs are disappearing.

VI. Developing Reading Skills

Read the sentences below, and write them in the correct order in the flowchart. When you are finished, go back to the reading and check your answers.

- Coral larvae are freely swimming.
- Polyps begin to clone themselves into a new, independent colony.
- Coral colonies form a coral reef.
- Coral larvae attach to submerged rocks or other hard surfaces.

1. Polyps release eggs into the water to mate.

↓

____

↓

____

↓

____

↓

____

VII. Vocabulary in Context

1. Fill in the blank with the **boldfaced** word or phrase from the reading that best completes each sentence. Change the form of the word if necessary.
   (1) Another mosquito-borne infection, dengue, is found primarily in urban and rural tropical and ______________ regions.
   (2) The movie's special effects failed to ______________ people.
   (3) The United States and China together produce well over one-third of the ______________ that causes climate change.

2. Choose a word or phrase that best completes each sentence.
   (1) Coal power stations ______________ toxic gases into the atmosphere.
   a. disrupt b. release c. provide d. sustain
   (2) Every day I have a "green drink," an herbal preparation containing numerous tonic substances like ginseng and also various forms of ______________ and chlorophyll extracts.
   a. fish b. algae c. larvae d. corals
   (3) Plants absorb ______________ during photosynthesis.
   a. sewage b. agrochemicals c. acid d. carbon dioxide

VIII. Grammar Point

Phrasal verb

A phrasal verb is a verb that is made up of a main verb together with a preposition or two. In most cases, their meaning is not obvious from the meanings of the individual words themselves.

For example:
She has always **looked down on** me.
They **broke up** a few years ago.
Take off your shoes before you walk in the room.

IX. Writing a Summary

A summary is a short paragraph that provides the most important information from a reading. It usually includes the main ideas, not details. When you write a summary, don't copy from the reading. Use your own words.

Write a summary of the passage. It should not be more than five sentences. The first sentences of the summary are given below. Write two or three more sentences to complete the summary.

Coral reefs are important to the economy and for the environment. Despite their importance, they have been threatened in recent years.

____

____

____

____

____

X. Topics for Discussion and Writing

1. What kinds of benefits do corals reefs provide to humans? What do coral reefs do for the environment? Talk about these with your classmates.

2. Beautiful, life-sustaining coral reefs are dying in many places all around the world. What do you think is the major cause of their dying? What can we do to protect them? Discuss these with your classmates.

Did You Know?

Ocean acidification is often referred to as osteoporosis of the oceans because as acidity rises, shell-building creatures such as lobster, oyster, crab, shrimp, and coral are unable to extract calcium carbonate from the water that they need to build their shells and are thus unable to survive.

- Philippe Cousteau, Jr.

Marine Pollution: Oil Spill Incidents

Unit 10

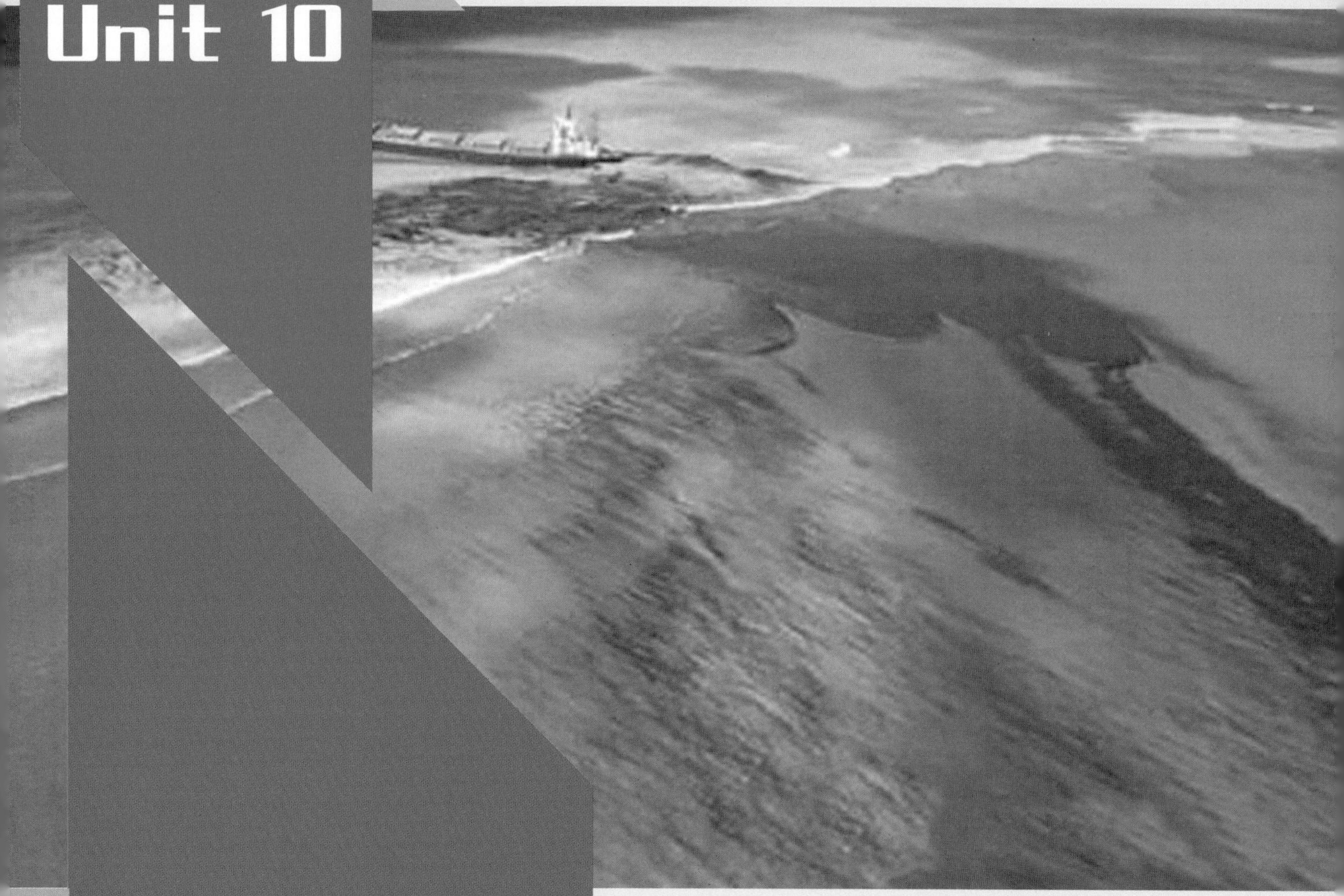

Source: Aug.8, 2020. YonhapNews

I. Pre-reading

photo by Mee Jee[May] Lee

1. Look at the oil spill map. How did this incident occur and what happened to areas of Mallipo Beach polluted by the country's worst-ever oil spill?
2. What is the major function of a water surface cleaner, as shown in the picture?
3. Look at the photos of the people on Mallipo Beach. What do you think the people are doing?

II. Vocabulary Preview

The following words appear in **bold** in the reading. Match each with its correct definition.

1. adopt	a. to raise to a higher degree
2. amend	b. to make a sudden, sharp, distinct sound
3. enhance	c. to make impure or unsuitable
4. collide	d. to accept or act in accordance with (a plan, principle, etc.)
5. snap	e. to strike against something with a forceful impact
6. seal	f. to close by any form of fastening that must be broken before access can be gained
7. contaminate	g. to alter, modify, rephrase, or change by formal procedure (a motion, bill, constitution, etc.)

III. Reading

Marine Pollution: Oil Spill Incidents

International shipping transports about 90% of global trade goods. You would not imagine the **vast** quantity of grain or coal being transported by airplane. Shipping offers a cost-effective means of transporting goods. The original task of the International Maritime Organization (IMO) was principally concerned with the safe operation of ships. However, with the 1954 International Convention for the Prevention of Pollution of the Sea by Oil (OILPOL Convention) taking effect in 1959, the IMO began assuming responsibility for the issues of pollution by ships. Over many years, the organization subsequently has **adopted** a broad range of measures to prevent and control marine pollution caused by ships. These measures have been successful enough to reduce marine pollution and to show the organization's **commitment** to marine environmental protection. Of the 51 treaty instruments for the regulations of international shipping adopted by the IMO, 21 directly address environmental issues. Thus the IMO can be said a specialized agency of the United Nations responsible for the prevention of marine pollution by ships as well as for the safety and security of shipping.

The Marine Environment Protection Committee (MEPC), consisting of all member states of the IMO, is one of the five main committees empowered to consider the prevention and control of pollution from ships and the adoption and **amendment** of conventions and other regulations and measures to ensure their enforcement. Marine pollution-related matters are mainly dealt with by the Marine Environment Division under the MEPC. The prevention of marine pollution by oil was its original focus, resulting in the adoption of the International Convention for the Prevention of Pollution from Ships (MARPOL) in 1973. This original MARPOL Convention has been amended over time to employ a much broader range of measures. It now

MARPOL 73/78's guidelines for the preservation of marine eco-systems

also includes requirements to specify pollution from chemicals, other harmful substances, sewage, garbage and under Annex VI adopted in 1997, air pollution and **emissions** from ships.

When petroleum or hazardous substances happen to be released into the sea by accident, they can severely impact the marine eco-systems. Not to mention the damage to fish and underwater organisms, oil spills destroy wildlife habitats on the coast. Oil spills also affect human lives. Due to its **expertise** in oil spill response, the U.S. Government is often asked to assist in responding to oil spill incidents that occur in other countries. Depending on the nature and location of the spill, the United States offers appropriate levels of assistance, especially when that assistance can **enhance** international relations and demonstrate a commitment to protecting the marine environment.

The MT Hebei Spirit's oil spill incident is known to be the worst oil spill that ever happened on the sea of South Korea with ongoing environmental and economic effects. The incident occurred on the morning of December 7, 2007, local time in the ocean off the west coast of South Korea. At about 7:30 a.m., a crane barge owned by Samsung Heavy Industries, being towed by a **tugboat**[1], **collided with** the Hebei Spirit. The Hong Kong registered crude-oil carrier was anchored at the time. After the cable linking it to the tugboat **snapped** in the rough seas, the crane barge was floating free. The

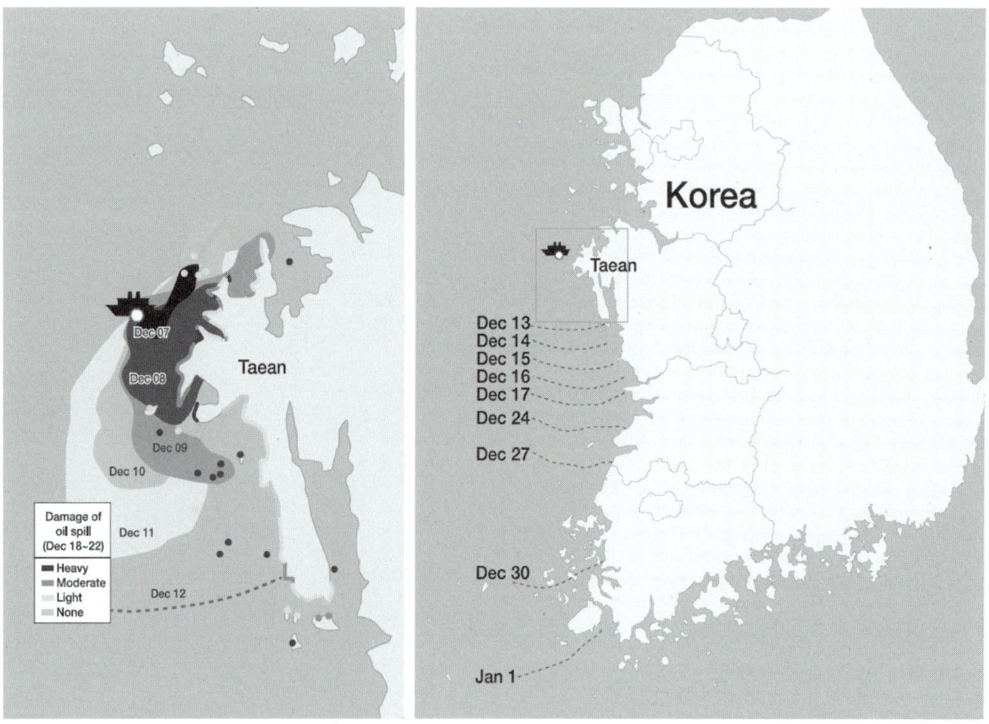

Spread of spilled oil and damage of oil spill along the shoreline at initial stage.

---

1) **Tugboat:** a small vessel fitted for towing; a powerful, strongly built boat designed to tow or push other vessels, and to assist in maneuvering a ship in a confined area

Hebei Spirit was carrying 260,000 tonnes of crude oil. The collision punctured three of the five tanks aboard the Hebei Spirit, resulting in the **leak** of about 10,800 tonnes of crude oil, although no **casualties** were reported. They pumped the remaining oil into the undamaged tanks and **sealed** the holes. The oil spill took place near Mallipo Beach in Taean County. Mallipo Beach is considered one of South Korea's most beautiful beaches. The region affected by the spill is one of Asia's largest wetland areas where **migratory** birds arrive. It involves 445 sea farms as well as a national maritime park.

On December 9, the oil **slick**[2)] was already 33 km long, 10 m wide, and 10 cm thick in some areas. Over half of the region's sea farms had lost their stocks and at least 30 beaches had been affected by the oil slick. The spill saturated Sinduri Dune, a South Korean natural treasure. Mallard ducks, seagulls, and other marine creatures were found tarred by the oil. Fortunately, most of the migratory birds had not yet visited the region. Otherwise, it could have resulted in much bigger demage, some said. By December 15, the oil slick had **contaminated** at least five beaches nearby with large tar lumps and then further made its way to Boryeong, commonly known as Daecheon, a city in South Chungcheong Province and to Gunsan in North Jeolla Province.

Oil spills leave not only costly but also potentially deadly impacts on the local fisheries and the aquatic environment. We know the unexpected can happen. The important thing is learning lessons from such disasters and having a good contingency plan in case of spillage or damage.

---

2) **Slick:** a smooth or slippery place or spot or the substance causing it

IV. Fact Check

Read the passage again and then read the following statements. Write a T if the statement is true and an F if false. If false, rewrite it to make it true.

1. _____ Seafarers deliver more than 90% of everything we eat, use and consume in many countries by sea.

2. _____ Even though many marine environment researchers argue that air pollution and emissions from ships as well as oil spills can severely impact marine ecosystems, the MARPOL Convention is still restricted only to the prevention of marine pollution by oil.

3. _____ Because of its expertise in treating oil spill incidents, the United States has helped many countries in plight.

4. _____ Several people were injured when a crane barge owned by Samsung Heavy Industries collided with the anchored Hong Kong registered crude-oil carrier, Hebei Spirit.

5. _____ Within eight days after the Hebei Spirit oil spill incident, the oil slick had made its way from Mallipo Beach in Taean County to Gunsan in North Jeolla province, resulting in many beaches being contaminated with large tar lumps.

V. Reading Comprehension

Choose the best answer for each question.

1. **What is the main idea of the passage?**
   a. The definition of MARPOL and the oil spill incidents subject to MARPOL
   b. The function of the IMO and the definition of MARPOL
   c. The amended versions of MARPOL and other international conventions regarding the prevention of marine pollution by ships
   d. The function of IMO and responsibilities of the United States

2. **Which of the following is not true of the MT Hebei Spirit at the time of the collision mentioned in the passage?**
   a. It carried around 260,000 tonnes of crude oil.
   b. The collision resulted in three of the five tanks being punctured.
   c. Around 10,000 tonnes of oil was spilled out.
   d. All the remaining oil from the damaged tanks leaked after a good while.

3. **Which of the following can be inferred from the passage?**
   a. The purpose of IMO's establishment was principally concerned with maritime safety only.
   b. The MARPOL convention is still limited only to the prevention of marine pollution by oil.
   c. The distance from the oil spill site is the principal element in the U.S. Government's decision to offer international aid.
   d. It took a month for most of the beaches in Taean County to be contaminated with large tar lumps.

4. **Which of the following is not one of amended requirements for the MARPOL convention?**
   a. the prevention of marine pollution by oil
   b. requirements addressing pollution from chemicals and other harmful substances
   c. requirements addressing pollution from garbage and sewage
   d. the prevention of air pollution and emissions from ships

5. Which of the following is **not** relevant to the incident of the MT Hebei Spirit oil spill?
   a. After the incident, seagulls, mallard ducks and other sea life inhabiting the polluted region were dying slowly because of being tarred by the oil.
   b. The incident occurred near the port of Mallipo on the Yellow Sea coast of Taean County on a winter morning in 2007.
   c. The region affected by the spill is home to one of Asia's largest wetland areas and also contains a national maritime park and more than 400 sea farms.
   d. Hong Kong registered crude carrier Hebei Spirit collided with the anchored crane barge owned by Samsung Heavy Industries.

VI. Developing Reading Skills

Read the passage again. Then complete the flowchart with accurate information from the passage.

1. Write keywords of the amendments made to the International Convention for the Prevention of Pollution from Ships (MARPOL) during following periods.

in 1973	from 1974 to 1996	in 1997
The prevention of marine pollution by oil		

⬇

2. When and how did the oil spill incident occur in Taean County, South Korea?

When	
How	

⬇

3. What happened in the polluted region over time?

After 2 days	
After 7 days	
After 8 days	

VII. Vocabulary in Context

1. Fill in the blank with the **boldfaced** word or phrase from the reading that best completes each sentence. Change the form of the word if necessary.

(1) The transport helicopter he was in ______ with another and crashed.

(2) Making a ______________ involves dedicating yourself to something, like a person or a cause.

(3) The university research team found that about 2.5 percent of the river's total flow was ______________ from the bottom of Lake Powell.

2. Choose a word or phrase that best completes each sentence.

(1) His group hopes that ship greenhouse gas __________ will fall 50 percent by 2050.

a. emissions b. casualties c. sewage d. lumps

(2) These guests are individuals who have vast experience and _________ in the topic being discussed.

a. novice b. expertise c. amateur d. commitment

(3) The __________ routes of birds extend to thousands of miles.

a. resident b. permanent c. vast d. migratory

VIII. Grammar Point

The subject of nonfinite -ing verbs called "gerunds" can be either in the
possessive case or in the object or common case where the subjects of main
clauses are different from those of gerund clauses as follows:

a. Would you mind **me/my** opening the window?
b. I objected to **him/his** being nominated.
c. I objected to **Perry's** being nominated.
d. The oil slick reached Anmyeon-do (Anmyeon Island), resulting in at least **five beaches** (not five beaches') being contaminated with large tar lumps.

Note that there are some exceptions to the use of the possessive as in (d). If the subject of the gerund is a plural noun, the common case is used, like (d). In addition, if the subject of the gerund is an inanimate noun, the commoncase is used as follows:

e. Some reviewers objected to **the book** (not book's) being subsidized.

IX. Writing a Summary

A summary is a short paragraph that provides the most important information from a reading. It usually includes the main ideas, not details. When you write a summary, don't copy from the reading. Use your own words.

Write a summary of the passage. It should not be more than five sentences. The first sentences of the summary are given below. Write two or three more sentences to complete the summary.

The major roles of the IMO were introduced for the purpose of discussing an international convention related to the prevention of marine pollution by ships. The passage also discusses when the MARPOL was first adopted and how it was amended over time due to marine pollution and air pollution by ship.

____

____

____

X. Topics for Discussion and Writing

1. A trial was held regarding compensation for damages caused by pollution resulting from the oil spill from the Hebei Spirit. Who won or lost the trial? If the fishermen's cooperative society in Taean County lost the trial, why do you think this happened?

2. Search for oil spill incidents that have occurred in Korea and discuss the cause and effect and oil spill responses with your classmates.

Did You Know?

Oil tanker spills are often the result of weather, equipment malfunction or human error. This type of oil spill often creates extreme natural disasters near coastlines as full tankers set to deliver their cargo.

Some of the worst maritime oil-tanker spills in history	
July 1979	Greek tanker Atlantic Empress spilled 287,000 tons off Trinidad and Tobago
March 1978	Amoco Cadiz spilled 223,000 tons off Brittany, France
April 1991	Cyprus based tanker, MT Haven spilled 145,000 tons off the coast of Genoa, Italy
November 1988	American owned tanker, The Odyssey spilled 132,000 tons off the coast of Nova Scotia, Canada.
November 2002	Greek-owned Prestige spilled 77,000 tons off Galicia, Spain
March 1989	Exxon Valdez spilled 37,000 tons in Prince William Sound, Alaska, US
December 2007	Hebei Spirit spilled 10,000 tons off S. Korea's west coast
April 2010	The Deepwater Horizon oil spill, caused by the explosion of the BP's oil rig in the Gulf of Mexico, leaked 780,000 tons of oil.

The world's worst recorded maritime oil spills were not the result of tanker disasters, however. Rather, oil well and rig disasters have spilled far more oil into oceans around the world.

Readings in Ocean Topics

Island Tourism and Its Problems

Unit 11

I. Pre-reading

1. Have you ever thought about why many tourists choose to travel to islands as their destinations?
2. How can we help solve some problems related with islands tourism?
3. Have you heard of the news regarding the island of Boracay in the Philippines in 2018? If so, can you explain what happened to this island?

II. Vocabulary Preview

The following words appear in **bold** in the reading. Match each with its correct definition.

1. indigenous	a. to lower in quality or value
2. implement	b. carry out, fulfill, to put into effect
3. degrade	c. third in place, order, degree, or rank
4. alter	d. originating, growing in a certain place or region
5. paramount	e. the act of combining or adding parts
6. integration	f. to change or make different; modify
7. tertiary	g. damaging, harmful
8. detrimental	h. of chief concern or importance

III. Reading

How can We Solve Problems of Island Tourism?

Travel allows us to discover some of the earth's most stunning natural wonders and diverse ecosystems. There are many beautiful islands to visit in different regions of the world. The mystique of islands ranges from different lifestyles and **indigenous** cultures to unique land formations, **flora and fauna**[1], and coastal resources. To keep that mystique alive, islands must **implement** sustainable tourism policies in such areas as environmental, economic, social, and cultural. With continuous development projects lacking proper management, however, they are going to be ruined and closed for visitors.

Unfortunately, new tourism development can **wreak havoc on**[2] natural scenery. When buildings are constructed and road paved over, it can **alter** the natural beauty of a place and **degrade** the overall visitor experience. The construction of tourism infrastructure in islands can damage local environments and wildlife. Forests are cleared, mangroves removed, and wetlands drained to **make way for**[3] hotels, piers, and golf courses. These changes of land use can also generate further environment damage, such as beach and soil erosion. When important habitats are destroyed by new tourism development, it threatens the survival of the wildlife inhabiting them. When tourism is not sustainable, it can harm and devastate the environments it relies on. We must take precautions to minimize our harmful impacts and protect the ecosystems. The prime tourist attractions in islands are mainly found on the coast such as beaches, sand dunes, and coral reefs that are easily damaged. The large amount of garbage created by tourism is a big problem.

The challenges to Island Tourism

Long term planning with **comprehensive** community and stakeholder input is becoming pivotal basis for tourism on islands. Plans also need to be value-based and reflect the indigenous culture and heritages. Long range planning must consider the balance of supply and demand of tourism.

First, it is a necessary part of the planning to empower the island community. Blueprints to protect and conserve the social and cultural

1) The flora and fauna of a place are its plants and animals.
2) to cause great damage
3) get out of the way for, or allow room for

structure are also important. Inspiring cultural pride through story-telling and memory of traditions, and a sense of identity are **paramount** for the community. This may involve the restoration of festivals, arts, language, and folklore and encouraging local residents to engage in activities. Efforts to sustain tourism in some islands found the meaningful **integration** of culture into the tourist experience difficult to achieve. It is challenging to achieve a balance of respect for the culture and provide tourists with the opportunity to learn about and **appreciate** the culture.

The education of tourists and locals is an important part to sustain islands. It is also very critical to empower the residents by educating and training them for their meaningful careers in the industry. This may involve facilitating education assistance because island residents do not always have comprehensive **tertiary** education programs in tourism. Residents also need to learn about the impact of tourism on their community. Education for tourists is also important because they need to learn about the unique cultural and historical aspects and features of the island.

Secondly, waste management and proper recycling program should be administered effectively. As an industry **prone to** overconsumption, tourism produces a substantial amount of waste and pollutants. In some places, tourists turn out up to twice as much waste as local residents. The waste problem can **put** incredible **strain on** local waste management system, causing landfills and sewage plants to overflow. The improper disposal of garbage, raw sewage, and toxic pollutants by tourists, hotels, and cruise ships is another major problem. This trash and pollutants can have **detrimental** effects on local people and wildlife. Therefore, not only are policies to keep the land and ocean unpolluted necessary, but waste management and recycling programs are also essential.

Alternative fuel sources will make the place more sustainable. Recycling programs are essential since tourists use much higher energy and fossil fuels than locals. While tourism contributes to the waste problem, the industry can also be part of the solution.

Thirdly, developers and tourists should make an attempt to reduce inequality among residents, and they should be educated on the importance of islands' relics and their heritage. Mass tourism development and disrespectful visitors can cause conflict with the local residents. Local residents may be marginalized by the tourism industry and their opinions not counted. Tourism can also **aggravate** income inequality and community hostility. Once the tourists visit the island, they need to be informed and guided regarding attractions, events, and tours.

Both developers and tourists should work together to ease the problems of islands tourism. Developers must be very concerned about planning and implementing the project. We as tourists must be conscientious and intentional in the way we travel if we want to change. When we travel without care or concern, we can cause irreparable damage to the environments and communities. But if we embrace practices for sustainability, we can combat some of the pressing issues and protect the destinations of island tourism.

IV. Fact Check

Read the passage again and then read the following statements. Write a T if the statement is true and an F if false. If false, rewrite it to make it true.

1. _____ To save and solve the issues of island tourism requires all parties of people to be involved.

2. _____ New construction should be taken into consideration to give more space to the residents.

3. _____ Political power groups in an island may boost rapid construction for tourism promotion.

4. _____ Various efforts should be put in to establish a sustainable environment in islands.

5. _____ The authorities of islands should offer some incentives for the use of alternative fuel.

V. Reading Comprehension

Choose the best answer for each question.

1. What is the purpose of the reading?
   a. To warn tourists of the possible danger in exploring islands
   b. To inform people of the effects of the development of islands and ways to prevent them
   c. To teach people how to deal with tourists' impact on the island tourism
   d. To promote island tourism and stimulate more investment

2. What is **not TRUE** about the reading?
   a. It is advised that the locals never feel disempowered in developing their island.
   b. Tourism may have the potential to both cause problems and come up with solutions in terms of waste issues.
   c. A conflict between tourists and the locals should be solved through the management of the tourism authorities.
   d. The issues of environmental sustainability present various aspects because islands have diverse geographical configurations and biological species.

3. What is **NOT** the reason for tourists to explore a new place for a visit?
   a. It can give them an opportunity to enjoy the beauty of nature.
   b. It can provide them with a variety of activities.
   c. It can offer some chance to experience culture and lifestyle of the indigenous people.
   d. It can offer some experience of learning how to rehabilitate the islands.

4. According to the passage, which party seems to be the main contributor to the waste problem in islands?
   a. developers
   b. local residents
   c. tourists
   d. island government authorities

5. According to the passage, what is **NOT** a way the author says to solve the challenges in developing island tourism?
   a. Empowerment of the locals should be maintained to ensure the success of the development.

b. The education of both tourists and locals is important to keep the islands sustainable.

c. Developers and tourists all work together to reduce the problems of the islands.

d. Local residents' equality should be addressed by both developers and tourists to alleviate possible internal conflicts.

VI. Developing Reading Skills

Finding the Topic and Main Idea

The *topic* of a piece of writing is its subject — what the writing is about. The main idea is the writer's message about the topics. The main idea is sometimes, but not always, stated directly in the text. Often you must infer the main idea from several sentences.

Example

In the last paragraph of the reading, the sentence "Both developers and tourists should work together to ease the problems of islands tourism." is the main idea.

VII. Vocabulary in Context

1. Fill in the blank with the **boldfaced** word or phrase from the reading that best completes each sentence. Change the form of the word if necessary.

(1) Some kids are ___________ letting their minds wander and daydreaming.

(2) Any military reaction would in turn hurt the nation's economy and _____________ the North Korea's ruler, Kim Jong-Eun.

(3) Studying for the final examination has put too much __________ on the students.

2. Choose a word or phrase that best completes each sentence.

(1) A ______________ rehabilitation approach takes into account all these factors.

a. detrimental b. comprehensive c. compliant d. degrading

(2) If these ______________ foods were indeed similar in food value to pine nuts, why are bears not already wolfing them down?

a. altercating b. atrocious c. allusive d. alternative

(3) The event teaches children to ______________ all types of art.

a. allure b. alleviate c. appreciate d. affiliate

VIII. Grammar Point

Allow A to B usage

When you use verbs such as **allow**, **encourage**, and **urge**, it is followed by **an objective** and **to infinitive form**:

Travel **allows** us **to discover** some of the earth's most stunning natural wonders and diverse ecosystems.

Ex) He **urged** me **to apply** for the scholarship for the first year students.
He **encouraged** all of his students **to work** hard for the final examination.

IX. Writing a Summary

A summary is a short paragraph that provides the most important information from a reading. It usually includes the main ideas, not details. When you write a summary, don't copy from the reading. Use your own words.

Write a summary of the passage. It should not be more than five sentences. The first sentences of the summary are given below. Write two or three more sentences to complete the summary.

We love to travel. Travel allows us to go and explore the unique beauty and culture of different places and people. But if we do not consider a smart travel, many islands would be ruined to the point where they cannot be restored. …

X. Topics for Discussion and Writing

1. What might be the better ways to work with the island residents in terms of developing plans to reduce garbage disposal?

2. What would you suggest as requirements for stakeholders when they initiate a new project to develop a new road system for an island?

Did You Know?

Did you know that on April 4, 2018, the government of the Philippines announced the closure of its most famous holiday island Boracay to tourists for six months to clean it up after concerns that rapid development and pollution was threatening its idyllic shores. President Rodrigo Duterte ordered the shutdown to regain its cleanness and purity. The tourism boom on Boracay brought jobs and investment but strained the island's water and rubbish disposal system and its sewer system. It reopened after a six-month rehabilitation project to local and foreign tourists. Now after the reopening, it remains one of the top beaches in Asia.

Unit 12

The Fourth Industrial Revolution and Autonomous Ships

I. Pre-reading

1. Are you worried that a robot will be able to do your job better than you do?
2. Although robots have been increasingly doing many of our jobs since the 1960s, why are politicians and business leaders only now becoming worried about robot usage causing mass unemployment?
3. Do you think self-driving cars and autonomous unmanned ships are safe and good for society?

II. Vocabulary Preview

The following words appear in **bold** in the reading. Match each with its correct definition.

1. blur	a. to make something last a longer time
2. demonstrate	b. to succeed in dealing with a problem or difficulty
3. prolong	c. to hold a weapon or tool that you are going to use
4. eliminate	d. to show or make something clear
5. wield	e. to prevent someone from paying full attention to something
6. surmount	f. to make the difference between two things less clear
7. distract	g. to completely remove or get rid of something

III. Reading

Fourth Industrial Revolution and Autonomous Ships

The current technological revolution has been fundamentally **altering** the way we live, work, and relate to one another. Scientists claim that the **transformation** can be unlike anything we have experienced before in its scale, scope, and complexity. No one is certain yet how the revolution will **unfold**, but one thing is clear that confronting it must be **integrated** and comprehensive, involving **stakeholders** from all walks of life.

The First Industrial Revolution was derived from the advent of mechanical production equipment operated by water and steam power. The Second achieved mass production by using electric power. The Third made it possible to automate production by utilizing electronics and information technology. Now, the Fourth Industrial Revolution (or Industry 4.0) is emerging out of the Third - the digital revolution that has been evident since the middle of the 20th century. Its main feature is a fusion of technologies that is **blurring** the lines between the physical, digital, and biological spheres.

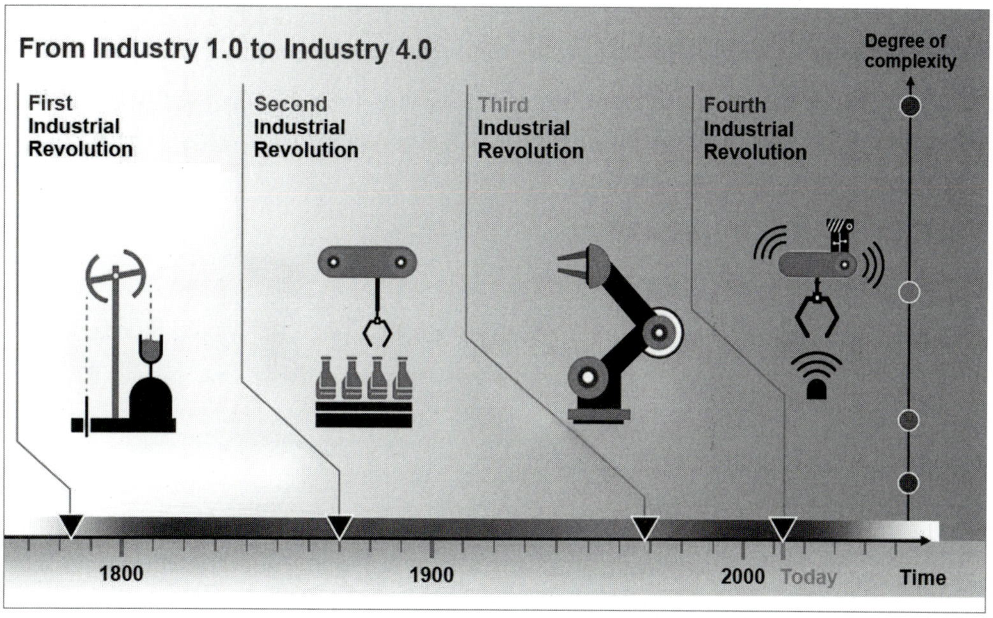

In terms of its speed, scope, and systems impact, the Fourth Industrial Revolution represents itself as not merely a **prolongation** of the Third, but as a distinctive one. The speed of current breakthroughs is unprecedented. Compared to previous industrial revolutions, the pace of the Fourth is **exponential**. The range of the changes created by **interrupting** almost every industry across the globe goes beyond anyone's imagination.

Arguably, the Fourth Industrial Revolution may substitute traditional ships with "smart ships" – either totally autonomous, unmanned, and remotely controlled from onshore stations or semi-autonomous with a skeleton crew on board. The unmanned ship is fully operational, going somewhere, and carrying something. Just like self-driving cars, remotely controlled autonomous ships will become available in the near future. Such autonomous ships can improve operational efficiency by ensuring optimal operation routes based on real-time weather and maritime conditions. Crew have always faced difficulties living on board for a long period at a time, but working conditions will be significantly improved in the future when fleets are managed from onshore control centers. Above all, the issue of crew shortages will be offset, leading to a decline in labor costs that currently account for the **lion's share** of total operation costs. These changes are not limited to the crew on board, however. The designs of ships will fully **evolve** as well. With no crew to accommodate, the deckhouse and safety design regulations for the crew can be **eliminated**, allowing future ships to be designed with larger cargo capacities.

File image courtesy Rolls-Royce Marine

In 2016, Rolls-Royce released a plan to develop an autonomous unmanned ocean-going ship by 2035. DNV-GL is developing an autonomous and fully battery-powered vessel, named ReVolt. According to Rolls-Royce, "Autonomous shipping is the future of the maritime industry. This is happening. **It is not if, it's when**."

The arrival of autonomous ships is beyond **dispute**. On December 3 2018, the world's first fully autonomous ferry was successfully **demonstrated** in Finland by Rolls-Royce and Finnish Finferries. The captain at a remote operating center, some 50 km away took control and navigated the vessel. The ferry was equipped with sensor fusion and collision avoidance utilizing artificial intelligence. Automatic berthing was also performed. It achieved all this without any human intervention. In the near future, a single

crew could conceivably operate 50 ships from a remote operations center. **High seas**[1] rescues could be carried out by joysticks **wielded** by operators thousands of miles away.

Is this realistic? Countless questions remain to be solved and no new age begins without sceptics. Who will fight a fire at sea? Who will respond to shifting cargo in **heavy seas**[2]? How will a structural failure be fixed? These are all pertinent questions, but there are those who believe that these technical barriers are **surmountable**. The IMO has begun a study of how regulations can accommodate autonomous shipping.

Unlike earlier innovations, the very idea of autonomous shipping directly challenges the notion of "seafarers-matter." Like the fate of cashiers, bank tellers, taxi drivers, and phone operators, the profession of seafarers can be eliminated by technology. On the other hand, autonomous ships, if fully evolved, would eliminate seafarer fatalities, just as fully evolved autonomous vehicles could theoretically save many people's lives each year **distracted** with texting or drinking while driving. With regard to saving seafarers' lives, however, as relatively fewer fatalities occur, the major justification for autonomous ships seems to be economic. Crew costs could be reduced, about 6% of total operating costs according to one estimate, while increasing vessel utilization as crew **quarters**[3] and support systems are converted into extra cargo **holds**[4]. Insurance and repair costs would similarly drop. Cost reduction in shipping and trade might result, but it is more problematic to see how the seafarer wins.

---

1) **High seas:** the open, unenclosed waters of any sea or ocean. In Law, "high seas" means the area within which transactions are subject to court of admiralty jurisdiction.
2) **Heavy sea:** a sea in which the waves run high
3) **Quarter:** living compartments, a room or cabin for officials on ship
4) **Hold:** the space below decks utilized for the stowage of cargo and stores in ships

IV. Fact Check

Read the passage again and then read the following statements. Write a T if the statement is true and an F if false. If false, rewrite it to make it true.

1. _____ The three precedent industrial revolutions can show us how the current progress of a technological innovation will change our life and work.

2. _____ The Fourth Industrial Revolution is not merely an extension of the Third Industrial Revolution but a distinctive and independent technological innovation.

3. _____ The operation of autonomous and unmanned ships can be compensated for with the decrease in crew and consequently the great reduction of labor costs.

4. _____ In the final month of 2018, the world's first fully autonomous ferry was successfully demonstrated in Finland.

5. _____ The full adaptation of autonomous ships will result in sudden and quick increase in insurance and repair costs.

V. Reading Comprehension

Choose the best answer for each question.

1. What is the main idea of the passage?
   a. The meaning of the Fourth Industrial Revolution and some responses to this technological innovation in the shipbuilding industry
   b. The definition of the Fourth Industrial Revolution and the effects of autonomous ships as its example in the shipping industry
   c. The arrival of the Fourth Industrial Revolution and its impact on business and government
   d. The arrival of the Fourth Industrial Revolution and the challenges and opportunities shaping the future of the maritime industry

2. What does the phrase "**lion's share**" mean in Paragraph 4?
   a. The largest portion
   b. The penny stock
   c. The king of farmland
   d. The leader of the forest

3. What does the phrase, "**It is not if, it's when.**" mean as mentioned in Paragraph 5?
   a. It's not a matter of "if," it's a matter of "when."
   b. "If" should not be used. Instead you should use "when" in that sentence.
   c. We cannot say "if" but we can say "when" in some cases.
   d. "When" is more important than "if" in this case.

4. Which of the following is NOT inferred, if autonomous ships are fully operated?
   a. They can save tens of thousands of crew lives annually, eliminating the human-caused maritime disasters.
   b. A single operator can theoretically navigate a large number of autonomous ships from a remote operations center.
   c. They can eliminate disasters resulting in death of seafarers.
   d. The deckhouse, crew cabins, and safety design on ship can be converted to hold more cargo.

5. Which of the following questions is not relevant to ones argued by sceptics about the new age of technological innovation?
   a. Who, in autonomous ships, will fight a fire at sea?
   b. Could high seas rescues be carried out by someone thousands of miles away?
   c. Who, in autonomous ships, will respond to shifting cargo in heavy seas?
   d. Like cashiers and bank tellers, will seafarers be eliminated by technology?

VI. Developing Reading Skills

Read the passage again. Then complete the flowchart with accurate information from the passage and from the picture below.

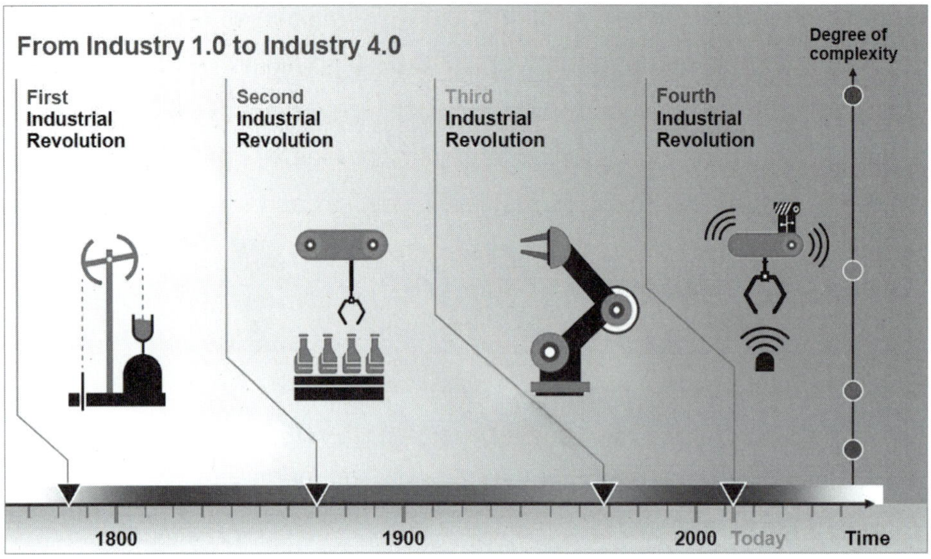

1. Write keywords of the four industrial revolutions.

1st	2nd	3rd	4th

⬇

2. Provide at least five general characteristics of the Fourth Industrial Revolution; The first is given to you as an example.

(i)	In its scale, scope, and complexity, the transformation will be unlike anything humankind has experienced before.
(ii)	
(iii)	
(iv)	
(v)	

⬇

3. How many examples and which features are provided in the passage to describe autonomous ships? Fill in the blank with your correct answers, as follows.

	Examples	Features
(i)	Rolls-Royce	1. In 2016, its plan was released. 2. Autonomous unmanned ocean-going ships will be developed by 2035.
(ii)		
(iii)		

⬇

4. Suggest some advantages and disadvantages of autonomous shipping to challenge the notion of "seafarers-matter."

Advantages	
Disadvantages	

VII. Vocabulary in Context

1. Fill in the blank with the **boldfaced** word or phrase from the reading that best completes each sentence. Change the form of the word if necessary.
   (1) Clinton and Bush together have more baggage than the cargo __________of a 747.
   (2) It is very important for the crew to get back into crew ________ and to rest.
   (3) The following is a dramatic comparison of linear and ________ growth.

2. Choose a word or phrase that best completes each sentence.

(1) As the story ______s, we learn more about William's childhood.

a. unfold b. integrate c. demonstrate d. dispute

(2) They would even take physical action. They said they would seize any tanker on the _________ seas loaded with Iraqi oil unless this issue is resolved.

a. deep b. ocean-going c. high d. heavy

(3) Climate change is already seriously ____________ our lives, hurting our health and damaging our economy.

a. evolving b. interrupting c. abandoning d. blurring

VIII. Grammar Point

Subordinating conjunctions are essential parts of complex sentences that include at least two clauses, with one of the clauses being main (independent) and the other being subordinate (dependent). They are called clause adverbials beginning with such words as *after, although, as, as if, as soon as, because, before, if, once, since, that, unless, until, when, where, in case (that), in order that.* A subordinate conjunction performs two functions within a sentence. First, it illustrates the importance of the independent clause. Second, it provides a transition between two ideas in the same sentence. The transition always indicates a place, time, or cause and effect relationship. In the following examples, the subordinating conjunctions are in bold for easy identification:

1. **After** the basement flooded, we spent all day cleaning up.
2. I don't want to go to the movies **because** I hate the smell of popcorn.
3. **Until** spring arrives, we have to be prepared for more snow.

IX. Writing a Summary

A summary is a short paragraph that provides the most important information from a reading. It usually includes the main ideas, not details. When you write a summary, don't copy from the reading. Use your own words.

Write a summary of the passage. It should not be more than five sentences. The first sentences of the summary are given below. Write two or three more sentences to complete the summary.

Characteristics of each of the first three industrial revolutions were described in brief. In the case of the Fourth industrial revolution, its several major characteristics were mentioned because this revolution is most essential to the reading and required more attention.

X. Topics for Discussion and Writing

1. There has been a good deal of discussion recently suggesting that unmanned, autonomous ships represent the future of the maritime industry. Find out where this sort of discussion has been made regarding the possibility of truly autonomous and unmanned ships making their own decisions using artificial intelligence and discuss this issue with your classmates. For example, EU-funded research, IMO supporting e-Navigation, the 2016 World Economic Forum at Davos, etc.

2. The shipbuilding industry is highly influenced by technological advances as well as environmental issues, increases in seaborne trade, the life cycle of ships, and changes in regulations. Shipbuilding companies will be able to increase their value through the development of key technologies for remotely controlled and unmanned ships, autonomous ships, and remote management. Korea is working to escalate the competitiveness of its shipbuilding and maritime industries through ICT convergence. In this sense, do you think that the shipbuilding industry in Korea will flourish again when Korea's three shipbuilding giants prepare for a new era of the Fourth industrial revolution?

Did You Know?

The twenty-foot equivalent unit (often TEU or teu) is an inexact unit of cargo capacity often used to describe the capacity of container ships and container terminals. It is based on the volume of a 20-foot-long (6.1m) intermodal container, a standard-sized metal box which can be easily transferred between different modes of transportation, such as ships, trains and trucks.

How many numbers of TEU can you count in the picture?

Two forty-foot containers stacked on top of two twenty-foot containers. These four containers represent 6 TEU.

Answers

UNIT 1

Vocabulary Preview

1. b 2. f 3. a 4. d 5. e 6. c

Fact Check

1. F: The Spaniards did not succeed in trading with the Indian people through the maritime route.
2. T
3. T
4. F: Bartholomeu Dias was the first European to reach the Cape of Good Hope.
5. F: Herodotus did not round Africa.

Reading Comprehension

1. c 2. a 3. d 4. d 5. b

Vocabulary in Context

1. (1) hemisphere (2) tribute(s) (3) sagas
2. (1) c (2) d (3) b

UNIT 2

Vocabulary Preview

1. c 2. b 3. d 4. e 5. a 6. f

Fact Check

1. T
2. F: An octant is half the size of a quadrant.
3. T
4. F: The astrolabe was developed in the Arab world. OR: The compass was developed in China
5. T

Reading Comprehension

1. b 2. a 3. d 4. c 5. c

Vocabulary in Context

1. (1) orient (2) buffeted (3) routinely
2. (1) a (2) a (3) b

UNIT 3

Vocabulary Preview

1. e 2. f 3. c 4. b 5. d 6. a 7. g

Fact Check

1. F: It is not stated in the reading.
2. T
3. F: It is not stated in the reading.
4. T
5. T

Reading Comprehension

1. d 2. c 3. a 4. d 5. d

Vocabulary in Context

1. (1) exquisite (2) exhilarating (3) enchant
2. (1) c (2) a (3) a

UNIT 4

Vocabulary Preview

1. f 2. e 3. a 4. b 5. c 6. d 7. g

Fact Check

1. F: Jangsaengpo Whale Museum displays artifacts related to modern whalking industry of Korea.
2. T
3. F: The legend of Yeonorang and Seonyo has been handed down in Pohang.
4. F: In 1855 four American whaler landed at Gangwon Province.
5. F: Dokdo was named 'Liancourt Rocks' after a French whaling ship.

Reading Comprehension

1. b   2. d   3. d   4. b   5. b

Vocabulary in Context

1. (1) shipwreck   (2) cetaceans   (3) occupation
2. (1) a   (2) d   (3) c

UNIT 5

Vocabulary Preview

1. d   2. b   3. e   4. a   5. c   6. g   7. f

Fact Check

1. T
2. T
3. F: Fish have it, but not mammals.
4. F: Marine mammals can get much larger because their skeletons do not have to support the weight.
5. T

Reading Comprehension

1. d   2. c   3. c   4. d   5. a

Vocabulary in Context

1 (1) blubber   (2) insulator   (3) storage
2 (1) a   (2) d   (3) b

UNIT 6

Vocabulary Preview

1. f   2. e   3. a   4. b   5. d   6. c

Fact Check

1. F: In ten years, more than 60 percent of all seafood for human consumption will come from aquaculture.
2. T
3. F: The white meat of fish is better than the red meat of livestock in reducing cholesterol levels in the blood.

4. T
5. F: The primary function of aquaculture is to develop the method of fish farming to increase the amount of seafood available worldwide.

Reading Comprehension

1. d 2. c 3. b 4. a 5. d

Vocabulary in Context

1. (1) endangered (2) contemporary (3) result in
2. (1) b (2) d (3) a

UNIT 7

Vocabulary Preview

1. b 2. a 3. d 4. c 5. f 6. e 7. g

Fact Check

1. T
2. T
3. F: 'Fishing down' means catching the smaller fish after depleting the larger fish.
4. F: 'By-fishing' refers to catching undergrown fish unintentionally.
5. F: Two percent of the ocean is protected.

Reading Comprehension

1. c 2. b 3. d 4. b 5. d

Vocabulary in Context

1. (1) flux (2) declared (3) predatory
   (4) depleted
2. (1) a (2) c (3) a

UNIT 8

Vocabulary Preview

1. e 2. c 3. a 4. f 5. b 6. d

Fact Check

1. T
2. F: Scuba divers carry air tanks on their back to breathe.
3. F: A BC jacket is the main diving accessory that controls divers' buoyancy.
4. F: The deeper we go, the more nitrogen our body accumulates.
5. T

Reading Comprehension

1. b 2. c 3. d 4. b 5. a

Vocabulary in Context

1. (1) hypothermia (2) entangled (3) obviate
2. (1) d (2) c (3) a

UNIT 9

Vocabulary Preview

1. a 2. g 3. f 4. e 5. c 6. d 7. b

Fact Check

1. F: Aristotle classified corals as plant-animals.
2. T
3. F: Coral reefs live in not only shallow waters but also cold waters and even deep seas.
4. T
5. F: Coral bleaching has increased in recent years.

Reading Comprehension

1. b 2. d 3. a 4. b 5. c

Developing Reading Skills

Coral larvae are freely swimming. ⇒ Coral larvae attach to submerged rocks or other hard surfaces. ⇒ Polyps begin to clone themselves into a new, independent colony. ⇒ Coral colonies form a coral reef.

Vocabulary in Context

1. (1) subtropical (2) dazzle (3) pollution
2. (1) b (2) b (3) d

UNIT 10

Vocabulary Preview

1. d 2. g 3. a 4. e 5. b 6. f 7. c

Fact Check

1. T
2. F: The MARPOL has been amended many times, including requirements addressing pollution from chemicals, other harmful substances, garbage, sewage, air pollution and emissions from ships as well as the prevention of marine pollution by oil.
3. T
4. F: No casualties were reported at the incident.
5. T

Reading Comprehension

1. a 2. d 3. a 4. c 5. d

Developing Reading Skills

1. from 1974 to 1996: requirements addressing pollution from chemicals, other harmful substances, garbage, and sewage in 1997: the prevention of air pollution and emissions from ships
2. When: on the morning of 7 December 2007 local time

   How: A crane barge owned by Samsung Heavy Industries being towed by a tug boat collided with the anchored Hong Kong registered crude carrier Hebei Spirit
3. After 2 days: At least 30 beaches had been affected and over half of the region's sea farms were believed to have lost their stocks due to the spill. Sinduri Dune, a South Korean natural treasure, was reported to have been saturated by the spill.

   After 7 days: The oil balls had arrived at Anmyeon-do (Anmyeon Island), resulting in at least five beaches being contaminated with large tar lumps.

   After 8 days: The tar lumps had also floated to Boryeong (mostly around Wonsan Island and Sapsi Island of Boryeong) and to Gunsan in North Jeolla province.

Vocabulary in Context

1. (1) collided (2) commitment (3) leaking

2. (1) a (2) b (3) d

UNIT 11

Vocabulary Preview

1.d 2. b 3. a 4. f
5. h 6. e 7. c 8. g

Fact Check

1. T
2. F: Not stated
3. F: Not stated
4. T
5. F: Not stated

Reading Comprehension

1. b 2. c 3. d 4. c 5. A

Vocabulary in Context

1. (1) prone to (2) aggravate (3) strain
2. (1) b (2) d (3) c

UNIT 12

Vocabulary Review

1. f 2. d 3. a 4. g 5. c 6. b 7. e

Fact Check

1. F: We do not know how the current progress of a technological innovation will change the way we live and work because it has no historical precedent.
2. T
3. T
4. T
5. F: The full adaption of autonomous ships will make insurance and repair costs suddenly and quickly decrease in value or amount.

Reading Comprehension

1. b 2. a 3. a 4. a

Developing Reading Skills

1. 1st: water and steam power to mechanize production
   2nd: electric power to create mass production
   3rd: electronics and information technology to automate production
   4th: cyber-physical systems
2. (ii) It is characterized by a fusion of technologies that is blurring the lines between the physical, digital, and biological spheres.
   (iii) The speed of current breakthroughs has no historical precedent.
   (iv) When compared with previous industrial revolutions, the Fourth is evolving at an exponential rather than a linear pace.
   (v) It is disrupting almost every industry in every country. And the breadth and depth of these changes herald the transformation of entire systems of production, management, and governance.
3. (ii) DNV-GL. An autonomous and fully battery-powered vessel, named ReVolt is developing.
   (iii) The Yara Birkeland, Norway. (1) The world's first autonomous electric cargo ship will sail test voyages off the coast of Norway in 2018. (2) By 2019 it will be controlled remotely and it will be fully automated by 2020.
4. Advantages:
   (1) Just like fully adapted autonomous vehicles, fully adapted autonomous ships will save seafarer fatalities.
   (2) They could reduce crew costs, insurance and repair costs
   Disadvantages:
   Just like fully adapted autonomous vehicles, fully adapted autonomous ships will bring about mass unemployment.

Vocabulary in Context

1. (1) holds (2) quarters (3) exponential
2. (1) a (2) c (3) b